# Essays on Religion

# ESSAYS ON RELIGION

*Georg Simmel*

**EDITED AND TRANSLATED BY**

*Horst Jürgen Helle in collaboration with Ludwig Nieder*

*Foreword by Phillip E. Hammond*

*Yale University Press    New Haven and London*

Published by arrangement with the Society for the
Scientific Study of Religion Monograph Series, as
volume 10 in the series.

Copyright © 1997 by Yale University.
Designed by Sonia L. Scanlon.
Set in Bembo type by Tseng Information Systems,
Inc., Durham, North Carolina.
Printed in the United States of America by Book-
Crafters, Inc., Chelsea, Michigan.

Library of Congress Cataloging-in-Publication Data
Simmel, Georg, 1858–1918.
　　Georg Simmel, essays on religion / Georg
　　Simmel; edited and translated by Horst Jürgen
　　Helle in collaboration with Ludwig Nieder.
　　　　p.　　cm. — (Monograph series / Society for
　　the Scientific Study of Religion; no. 10)
　　　　Includes bibliographical references and index.
　　　　ISBN 0-300-06110-2 (alk. paper)
　　　　1. Religion.　　2. Religion and sociology.
　　I. Helle, Horst Jürgen.　　II. Nieder, Ludwig,
　　1959–.　　III. Title.　　IV. Series: Monograph series
　　(Society for the Scientific Study of Religion);
　　no. 10.
BL60.S5477　　1997
200—dc20
95-51112
CIP

A catalogue record for this book is available from
the British Library.
10　9　8　7　6　5　4　3　2　1

# Contents

Georg Simmel's friend Max Weber described himself as "religiously unmusical." Simmel, by contrast, was religiously very musical, as readers of these essays will discover. This figure of speech is extraordinarily appropriate here not only because Simmel frequently uses musical allusions in his analysis of religion but also because Simmel's notion of religion—what he calls piety or religiousness—is one of sensitivity *to* or capacity *for* religion. This sensitivity or capacity is very much what these essays are about.

In describing himself as unmusical in regard to religion, Weber obviously was not claiming that he was unknowledgeable about religion. Rather, he was saying, the religious experiences of others—experiences he understood and analyzed with great empathy—were experiences for which he himself lacked the capacity. Not so with Simmel! The "stuff" of religion was precisely what occupied Simmel's attention when he turned his analytic skills to that arena. He was not interested in religion as it is commonly understood—when it appears, as Simmel says, in "certain substantial forms"—but instead in that "particular spiritual quality" or "attitude of the soul" which precedes the forms of religion and which may or may not be projected onto such forms. "Just as causality does not create cognition but instead cognition creates causality," says Simmel, "so religion does not create religiousness but religiousness creates religion." Unlike Weber, then, Simmel had an outstanding "ear" for religiousness, and the subject matter of these essays reflects that.

English-speaking scholars can perhaps be forgiven for not yet appreciating Simmel's insights into religion. A 1905 issue of the *American Journal of Sociology* contained a translation of an essay on religion by Simmel that appears here in new translation as Chapter 9, "A Contribution to the Sociology of Religion." The essay was reprinted in abridged form in J. Milton Yinger's 1957 reader on the sociology of religion. In 1959 there appeared an awkward translation of Simmel's 1906 monograph; the considerably revised 1912 version appears here as Chapter 11, the longest of these essays. Other items previously published in English were Peter Etzkorn's translation of "The Conflict in Modern Culture" (1968) and Eleanor M. Miller and Dale J. Jaffe's translation of "On Religion from the Point of View of the Theory of Knowledge" (1984). Apart from these four pieces, however, Simmel's texts on religion have until now been available only to those who could read German. Even in present-day Germany, it seems, Simmel's essays on religion are not widely known, a situation that the German edition of these essays is designed to correct.

I always admired the little I knew of Simmel's writings on religion. Occasionally I included some discussion of him in my teaching, regretting that the small monograph was so difficult for students to read as to make it unusable. Imagine my interest, then, when I discovered during a visit to Horst Helle's seminar in June 1988 in Munich that he was preparing these essays for German publication. Why not translate them for English publication as well? I made the suggestion because I knew Helle's command of English. And why not, I suggested further, see if the Society for the Scientific Study of Religion (SSSR) would be interested in publishing the English edition as part of its Monograph Series? The response all around was positive. Moreover, the representatives of the SSSR agreed that general interest in Simmel's writings on religion extends well beyond sociology scholars, thus making advisable a joint publication with a press better able to market the book widely. Hence the happy collaboration with Yale University Press. Not only sociologists of religion but all students of religion will benefit from the publication of this book. I record here my admiration for Horst

Helle's undertaking and report with some pride my modest role as midwife. May Georg Simmel gain the recognition he deserves from the English-speaking community of religion scholars!

Phillip E. Hammond

The clinic chief is pleased with the intern's performance. In predicting a successful career, he summarizes his evaluation of the young physician: "He has the right attitude." The experienced M.D. in this little story takes his junior colleagues' scientific scholarship and technical know-how for granted, but he distinguishes them by the personal outlook that each one brings to bear in his or her professional work. Healing others remains intrinsically a service; yet socialization in schools and universities today does not necessarily emphasize the willingness to serve others. That is why in hospitals, as elsewhere, the *subjective factor*—attitude, and as a consequence the person's *perspective* on reality—makes a highly significant difference.

Georg Simmel recognized the increasing importance of the subjective factor in society a century ago: people with a high standard of living generally have more options than did their less-privileged forebears. As a result, their attitude—whether optimistic or pessimistic—has more impact on their construction of reality than it would if they had less freedom or fewer choices. At the same time, many persons living in highly industrialized societies share the frustration that stems from alienation from a world that seems to have its own independent existence, in disregard of the humans who brought it into being. The general and unpleasant tendency of social forms to become self-serving is demonstrated convincingly by Simmel when he studies the big city. In his famous lecture "The Metropolis and Mental Life," first published in 1903, he reminds us that "the development of modern culture is characterized by the predominance of what one can call the objective spirit over the subjective" (Simmel [1903] 1971, p. 337). Simmel notices that particularly during the nineteenth century the amplification of objective culture as "embodied in things and in knowledge" has outpaced "the cultural progress of the individual" (p. 337). Isolated urban subjects cope with overexposure to a horrendous objective reality through a "blasé outlook" (p. 329), indifference, and even aversion.

In view of Simmel's analysis of early industrialism ("Metropolis and Mental Life," 1903), further widening of the gap between the subjective and the objective was to be expected. The experience of living in isolation, surrounded by strange objects and outlandish persons, would intensify our need to bridge the chasm. Hope in culture—in art and religion as well as in scholarship—remains, and it is not surprising that Simmel turned to the study of these phenomena as a source of relief. During the last two decades of his life, from 1898 to 1918, he devoted a considerable part of his writing to the topic of religion.

In the texts presented here, Georg Simmel does not describe religion as a finite province of reality, like government or the economy; rather he treats it as an *attitude* or a *perspective*—a way of looking at the world as a whole. Yet he does not reduce religion to a set of subjective emotions that occur only within the individual; to him, religion, like art, constitutes a third realm, which exists between the subject and the object. It "is always an objectification of the subject and therefore has its place beyond that reality which is attached to the object as such or to the subject as such" (Simmel [1916] 1919, p. 29). Simmel sees reality as divided between the subjective and the objective, but a rift need not occur between the two: the third realm, created through the interaction of human beings, may serve as a bridge. Thus each religious person is somewhat of a pontifex—a bridge builder—insofar as he or she contributes to its construction. After all, that is what *religion* means, at least according to the etymology that has been handed down since Augustine's day: the Latin word *religare* implies a tying back together of what has been torn asunder.

To Simmel's first methodological tool, viewing religion not as an ensemble of beliefs but as a specific *attitude* or *perspective*, he adds, as we have mentioned, a second: treating religion as a reality capable of *bridging the rift* between the subjective and the objective. In addition, Simmel uses yet a third heuristic device: the *dialectic of form and content*. According to him, history advances through a process in which form and content are transmuted into one another. Continuity in history would not be possible if the same content (government, for example) did not appear in different forms (aristocracy, dictatorship, democracy), and unless the same form (autocratic leadership) were to shape various contents (family, state, church). Thus what appears as form and what as content depends on the perspective. If the religious perspective is taken, it can help recreate a wide variety of contents in the form of religious experiences.

Simmel points out that the idea of God may become the content of either the form *pious meditation* or of a quite different form: *intellectual reflection*. In the first, Simmel sees a religious phenomenon because of the form of piety. In the second, however, the form of rational analysis would prevent it from being recognized as a religious phenomenon, even though the content is the idea of God. In order to clarify that distinction even further, Simmel makes a distinction from 1902 on between *religion* and *religiosity*. If a person deals with contents that are taken from objectified religion in a scientific way, it may have no religious effect on his or her life, because religiosity may be absent.

Simmel illustrates this point in Chapter 10, his 1902 essay "Contributions to the Epistemology of Religion," with the prayer for faith. From the perspective of rational argumentation it is utterly pointless to pray for faith, because such a prayer would presuppose the existence of a deity—a deity, moreover, who has the power to hear and fulfill the prayers. Accordingly, the person praying would be asking for insight into a reality that is already assumed as given. Simmel, however, defines faith as the individual's ability to give *content* from objective *religion* the *form* derived from personal *religiosity*. To pray for a certain mental makeup or, in Simmel's terms, to pray for *religiosity* is then entirely plausible, either because the individual may feel the need for the deity to intervene on that issue or because the very practice of praying may produce the desired effect of making a pious frame of mind habitual.

Along with *form* and *content,* another important pair of terms is *center* and *periphery.* Simmel writes (and, as was typical for his time, he wrote *man* to imply both the male and the female form of humanity): "Man is free to the extent that the center of his being determines its periphery." What is unique and utterly personal would fill the center; that which many people have in common can be only peripheral to the individual. Simmel observes that Christian churches have tended to emphasize that which all or many believers have in common rather than encouraging each soul to let its talents bear fruit, according to Matthew 25: 26–27.

Simmel dramatizes this point in Chapter II, the 1912 edition of his monograph "Religion," when he quotes from Martin Buber's collection of tales from the Hasidim the story of a miracle-working Galician rabbi named Meir, who is supposed to have said to his pupils: "If the Lord asks me in the hereafter: 'Meir, why did you not become Moses?' I will reply: 'Because I am only Meir, Lord.' And if he goes on to ask me: 'Meir, why did you not become Ben Akiba?' I will also reply: 'Because I am simply Meir, Lord.' But if he asks me: 'Meir, why did you not become Meir?' what shall my answer be then?" This beautiful tale captures the fear of living outside one's center by filling one's life with peripheral activities.

Simmel has high regard for pious people and mystics, whose abilities and activities he very clearly distinguishes from those of scholars. As a sociologist of religion and as a philosopher of religion, Simmel believes that neither he nor anybody else has a mandate to make any learned statement about what may exist in the beyond. That is the realm of belief. As a result, in his writings on religion Simmel takes care not to confound the transcendent views that a certain religious *community* may summarize as its written creed with the subjective impressions that may shape the predispositions of the pious *person*. These two are potentially independent realities. As we have seen, religion as co-created by the interaction of believers is a third. This last is the central area of study for the sociology of religion.

Anyone whose interest has led him to look for early literature on the sociology of religion will inevitably be reminded of Max Weber's (1904) study *The Protestant Ethic and the Spirit of Capitalism*. Other classics in sociology also have added considerable weight to the study of religion: for example, Emile Durkheim's book *The Elementary Forms of Religious Life* (1912). Before him, Auguste Comte (1842) wrote about religious consciousness as the first of the three stages in which he believed human thought to have developed. Karl Marx (1844) referred to religion as a symptom of a lack of emancipation, and as the "opium of the people." Most experts on the sociology of religion will cite Comte, Marx, Durkheim, and Weber immediately as authors who wrote about religion, whether as a driving force (Max Weber) or as a hindrance to social change (Karl Marx). Only a very few, however, know of Georg Simmel's writings on religion. It is the aim of this book to draw attention to Simmel's contribution and to help give his work on the subject the place it deserves in the literature. In addition, the editor hopes to familiarize the reader with Simmel's singular understanding of religion and Simmel's own preoccupation, religiosity.

Georg Simmel lived from 1858 to 1918. Until 1914 he made his home in Berlin. He spent the last four years of his life, however, which coincided with World War I, as a full professor at the University of Strasbourg. He died there of liver cancer on September 26, 1918. Simmel, a Berliner, was of Jewish origin, belonged to a Protestant church, and became a philosopher and sociologist. He grew up as the youngest of seven children and received a sizable inheritance after the premature death of his father. This, and after 1900 his tenured position as associate professor (Extraordinarius) at the University of Berlin, allowed him to pursue his natural inclination toward intellectual autonomy.

Simmel earned his doctoral degree from the University of Berlin, which enjoyed considerable international reputation during the second half of the nineteenth century. Among the intellectuals who came from abroad to study in Berlin were George Herbert Mead and Robert Ezra Park. In Berlin, as well as elsewhere in Germany, Austria, and other parts of Europe, it has been—and to some degree still is—the tradition not to promote a scholar from within the department to the rank of full professor. This custom, intended to discourage intellectual inbreeding, excluded Simmel from eligibility for a professorship at the university where he had been a student, a Ph.D. candidate, and a *Privatdozent*. That is one of the reasons Max Weber tried to get him a professorship at Heidelberg; he failed, probably because of anti-Semitic prejudice there.

As a teacher without the rank of full professor at the university, Simmel was in competition with Eduard Zeller and Wilhelm Dilthey, who were both professors at the Philosophy Faculty; Simmel seems to have been the most inspiring and the most compelling lecturer of the three. A witty remark, which Simmel made in a very small group, nevertheless made the rounds. He was quoted as saying that apart from himself, two other philosophers were teaching at the University of Berlin, one called Zeller, who had no idea what philosophy was, and the other, Dilthey, who knew what it was but kept it a secret from everybody else.

While many admired Simmel both as teacher and as an insightful interpreter of the fundamental changes occurring in culture and society, he never generated a large and stable coterie. Instead, he was disowned by the devout Jews because of his membership in a Christian church; distrusted by conservatives because of his rejection of historical materialism as documentation (even though he used it as a heuristic tool); and considered suspect by Marxists because he rejected historical materialism as documentation and also because he considered Karl Marx a poor philosopher. In addition, many intellectuals who, like Schopenhauer, had turned to Buddhism felt alienated by Simmel's conclusion that Buddhism was not a religion at all because it lacked a personal god. Many Catholic intellectuals approved of Simmel's writings until they stumbled on the dilemma posed by the unremittingly critical teachings of Pius X against modernism, beginning in 1907. Simmel's ideas were not far removed from the "modernist" viewpoint that met with papal condemnation. Late in his life, Simmel abandoned the Protestant church. It was his fate and calling as scholar to stand alone.

He could have formed a close alliance with the most influential Jewish philosopher of the twentieth century, Martin Buber (1878–1965), who studied under both Simmel and Dilthey and who was not affected by these prejudices. Buber was familiar with Simmel's essays on religion, which had been published starting in 1898. As a result, he tried to persuade Simmel to write a monograph for his own series of essays, to be titled "Die Gesellschaft" (Society). The resulting text, "Die Religion," was first published in 1906, then revised and enlarged for the second edition of 1912. It appears here as Chapter 11, the longest in this collection.

Between the first essay on the topic, "Zur Soziologie der Religion" (A contribution to the sociology of religion), published in 1898 and included here as Chapter 9, and the first edition of the book *Die Religion* in 1906 came four important publications, although one of these was a slightly revised translation of another of them. In his introduction to an English-language anthology originally published in 1950, Kurt H. Wolff (1964) referred to an essay by Simmel (1903a) on the epistemology of religion, published in French. E. M. Miller and D. J. Jaffe apparently picked up on this reference and published a translation of the French text in 1984 (Miller and Jaffe 1984). In their introduction they recall that Simmel was in Paris for the World Exhibition in 1900 and that he lectured at the First International Philosophy Congress on religion from the epistemological perspective.

Among the participants at the congress were Herbert Spencer, Gabriel Tarde, Ferdinand Tönnies, Wilhelm Wundt, and Henri Bergson (Miller and Jaffe 1984, pp. 62ff.). Two texts resulted from the Paris lecture: in 1902 the "Beiträge zur Erkenntnistheorie der Religion" (Contributions to the epistemology of religion), Chapter 10 in this collection, and the French version of 1903.

In that same year Simmel's "Vom Heil der Seele" (On the salvation of the soul, 1903b) was published, which appears here as Chapter 4. The last of the four pieces produced between 1898 and 1906 is "Die Gegensätze des Lebens und die Religion" (Religion and the contradictions of life), which was published in 1904 and appears here as Chapter 5.

Kurt Wolff's selection of texts brought Simmel to the English-speaking specialists' attention. Soon after Donald N. Levine had earned his doctorate at the University of Chicago in 1957 with a dissertation comparing Simmel with Talcott Parsons (Levine 1957), Curt Rosenthal completed an English translation of *Die Religion,* titled *Georg Simmel: Sociology of Religion* (Rosenthal 1959). Although this translation was a pioneering work in some respects, it generated criticism both because it used the first edition of 1906 rather than the enlarged edition of 1912 and because the English rendition was awkward (Wolff 1963).

The 1912 version differs from the first edition in a complex way: it contains both additions and deletions, which are not merely editorial improvements but modifications in the argument. In Chapter 11 we have placed portions of the text that were added in the 1912 edition in brackets to make it possible for the reader to identify them.

Following the texts of 1898, 1902, 1903, and 1904, Simmel published four more short essays: "Das Christentum und die Kunst" (Christianity and art, 1907), Chapter 7; "Religiöse Grundgedanken und Moderne Wissenschaft: Eine Umfrage" (Fundamental religious ideas and modern science: An inquiry, 1909), Chapter 1; and the two texts first published in 1911, "Die

Persönlichkeit Gottes" (The personality of God), Chapter 6, and "Das Problem der religiösen Lage" (The problem of religion today), Chapter 2.

This collection presents as Chapter 8 a text that is not included in our German edition: "Rembrandts religiöse Kunst" (Rembrandt's religious art). This essay was printed in two parts by the daily Frankfurt newspaper *Frankfurter Zeitung*, on June 30 and July 1, 1914. Chapter 3 is the final part of the frequently cited lecture "Der Konflikt der modernen Kultur" (The conflict of modern culture), published in 1918, the year Simmel died. With the 1914 text added to this collection, the reader can safely assume that everything Simmel wrote explicitly on religion is included here. Needless to say, Simmel refers to religious phenomena in many of his other writings.

In this book Simmel's essays on religion have been arranged thematically rather than chronologically by Ludwig Nieder. The editor hopes that this grouping into five parts will make it easier for the reader to become familiar with Simmel's ideas. Most footnotes in the texts were added by the editor; footnotes written by Simmel are so indicated throughout the volume. Paragraphs in this edition do not necessarily correspond to those in the German.

Even though this introduction is intended to assist the reader in working with the texts by Simmel rather than to delay that activity, a number of acknowledgments are in order here. Phillip E. Hammond has written the foreword. In it, however, he grossly understates his own contribution: he and I worked on some of the texts at his home in Santa Barbara, sometimes spending as much as half an hour on a single crucial sentence. The Society for the Scientific Study of Religion has made this project its own. My gratitude goes to its former president Eileen Barker of London and to the past and present officers of the society.

The publisher of the German edition, Norbert Simon of Duncker & Humblot, Berlin, gave the idea of an English version his blessings with the kind idealism that has become rare among publishers. Allan Auld of Baker & Harrison Translations, Munich, struggled patiently and very successfully with Simmel's multidimensional syntax. Leonard Broom, the first to read the entire translation, impressed on us the need to make two or three manageable English sentences out of each of Simmel's extended statements. Eva M. Helle has reviewed the translation. Ludwig Nieder compared the different versions of the translation with Simmel's original texts, inserted additional chapter headings, and coordinated the work at the computer. Under his patient direction, several graduate students in the department at Munich got involved. Ludwig Nieder disciplined them with this singular threat: "If you do not do this properly, I will do it myself!" No matter how devoted the students were to their work, he frequently had to do the typing himself anyway. Finally Karen Feinberg put a large amount of work into editing the text and improved it immensely.

I am deeply grateful to everyone who supported this project. Whatever the virtues of this edition of Georg Simmel's texts, they are due largely to these persons' competent cooperation. The shortcomings are mine; I fervently hope that Simmel will not turn over in his grave, but that more and more social scientists will acknowledge his pathbreaking work.

Horst Jürgen Helle

**PART 1**  *Religion and Modernity*

*Fundamental Religious Ideas and Modern Science: An Inquiry [1909]*

The difficulties that currently beset religious life are caused by the conflict between religiousness as an inner state or need of man and all the traditional lore that, as the content of that inner state, offers itself as a means to fulfill these needs. It is not in fact because of science and scholarship that the dogmatic substance of religion has fallen prey to unbelief, if we take science to mean the methodical, precise investigation of facts and possibilities. A child born of a virgin, water transformed into wine, the resurrection and ascension to heaven of a deceased man: none of this has become less probable as a result of nineteenth-century science than it was according to the experience of people living in the thirteenth century. It is not so much specific facts on which science has cast light, because such knowledge has not really been relevant to religion, but rather the general scientific-intellectual mood of the times that poses a serious challenge to such dogmas. If historical inquiry has taught us that the virgin birth of the Redeemer, his divine sonship, the symbolism of the Last Supper, and much else that allegedly was specifically Christian are all part of an ancient ethnic imagery, this by no means destroys the subjective, or indeed the objective, religious significance of these traditions. For the fact of being able to understand developments in a historical sense does not prevent us from singling out one particular event, which is scarcely distinguishable from the rest in empirical terms, and attaching to it a quite unique transcendental significance—just as the same words, with apparently slight alterations, can express both something quite banal and a profoundly significant thought.

It has also long been accepted that the concept of God is unassailable from a scientific point of view. This much cannot be disproved: that the complexity of existence as a whole is created and fashioned by a superior power, with science merely enabling us to know of the relationships between the parts of this whole; and that alongside or among all the forces we know to be at work in the world, one other factor—the will of God—is constantly at work to preserve our existence. Not only can all of this not be disproved; it is also completely outside the sphere of scientific interest. Apart from certain details that do not affect the essential core of Christianity, it is not possible to produce any effective counterevidence to disprove religious lore using results produced by the exact sciences. As already suggested, however, it is certainly true that an adherence to the traditional content of religion is prevented by the spirit of science as a whole, by the application of basic scientific attitudes to what is not investigable, and by the tendency to define as believable reality only that which is scientifically probable.

It would be complete delusion, however, if one were to regard the inner needs that such lore has fulfilled until now as having died out along with the lore itself. There is absolutely no question that these needs cannot be silenced or diverted for anything more than a brief, transitory period: our knowledge of history shows that they have been rooted in human nature too long and too deeply. At least an extremely large section of civilized society is confronted with the problem of feeling a new urgency to satisfy certain inner needs—needs that seemed identical to the fulfillment provided for them in the past, and which therefore appeared to vanish momentarily when the illusory nature of this fulfillment was realized, leaving man with these needs in a complete void.

It is impossible to judge today how this problem will be solved. On the one hand, there are still those who claim that the victory of the spirit of science over the content of religion has eliminated religious needs; on the other hand, those who advocate the truth of such content struggle desperately to assert it, drawing on the support of all official authorities. We may well need to realize that religiosity is a particular *being,* a functional quality of humanity, so to speak, which entirely determines some individuals and exists only in rudimentary form in others. This fundamental feature will usually lead to the development of *articles of faith* and to the adoption of a transcendental reality, but it is not necessarily bound indissolubly to man's religious nature and inclination. Just as an erotic person is always erotic in nature, whether or not he has created—or ever will create— an object of love, so too is a religious person always religious, whether or not he believes in a God.

What makes a person religious is the particular way in which he reacts to life in all its aspects, how he perceives a certain kind of unity in all the theoretical and practical details of life— just as the artist gives *his* own particular response to existence as a whole and fashions *his* own world from it, and the philosopher does likewise in his own way. Religiousness thus can be seen in this light: as a form according to which the human soul experiences life and comprehends its existence—a form, incidentally, that is subject to the kind of strict demands and ideals, beyond the subjective, which a more naive mind would associate only with some externally imposed code. Seen in this way, however, there clearly can be no conflict whatever between religiosity and science. For on the one hand, the latter is itself simply a way of comprehending the world and our existence in it; both religiosity and science are able to perceive and interpret life in its entirety, and the two are just as incapable of conflicting with each other, or even of crossing paths, as are cognition and matter in Spinoza's system, because each already expresses the whole of existence in its own particular language. On the other hand, any scientific criticism can destroy only certain specific ideas of faith to which the nature and needs of religion have given rise in various ways. There is no doubt that such criticism has had this effect, as outlined above, and thus has created the current state of perplexity in religious life. As long as religiousness creates its own *specific* content, which is in fact cognitive and thus is in competition with theoretical reflection, there is no hope of any major change.

It is especially unproductive to fall back on certain details of religion that supposedly constitute its ultimate and inalterable essence, while leaving open to criticism those specific elements of religion which are historically determined and fortuitous. As long as these remain images of concrete reality, objectivizations of the religious state of being that are not a part of this inner state itself, they will always be dogged by criticism. The only solution to this problem lies in evolutions of the religious condition, which, as I mentioned before, nobody today can predict with any measure of convincing probability. With this reservation in mind, it seems to me that a solution will depend on religion's leaving the transcendental world of ideas it has created for itself, just as pure forms of thought created rationalistic metaphysics, and returning to those unique impulses of life itself which are to the religious person the essence of his being, the intrinsic coloring and form of all his inner and outer existence.

Of course, these impulses will incorporate all the specific content that is a part of life; thus one certainly can speak of a religious worldview. But such a view does not consist in actual *knowledge* of things, experiences, or destiny: it consists in an organization of these according to individual values and needs, a reaction of the heart, which invests them with a direct, personal meaning. If religion is not a set of claims but a certain state of being—which is precisely what enables it to interpret and judge empirical phenomena—then it can no more be disproved by science than can any other state of being. It becomes refutable, however, as soon as its images of things become detached from this inner essence and instead become rigidified into a system of knowledge that somehow imitates the thought processes of science and thus is compelled to compete with the latter on its own terms, just as the church must compete with the state as soon as it adopts the state's forms.

The fact of the existence of religions is extremely disquieting for the person in today's world who is neither inwardly committed to an existing religion nor regards religion, with supercilious "sophistication," as a mere dream from which mankind is gradually awakening. Among the existing historical religions, of course, he may see enormous discrepancies in metaphysical depth and emotional makeup, in ethical adequacy and intellectual significance. These discrepancies, however, concern only the *content* of religious faith, not its fundamental position in relation to reality. As knowledge of the unknowable, as direct or somehow indirect experience of the metaphysical, there is no difference between Vitzliputzli and Ormuzd, between Baal and Wotan, between the Christian God and Brahman. If faith in any one of these is prevented by the question of whether or not they are real, the same obstacle applies to all of them. The modern-day person referred to above is convinced that we are stuck firmly in the empirical world, just as we are in our own skin, and that any attempt to jump out of it with our physical body would be as futile as trying to reach out to the world of the hereafter with the spiritual means at the disposal of our soul. For religious faith in a particular transcendental sphere does not permit any dilution; the content of faith must be real, as solid as we can possibly conceive—much more so than the empirical world.

We might admit that the empirical world itself is an "in my mind"; nonetheless, it is sufficient that this "idea" tallies with the criteria of our knowledge, and that our mental image of it causes the practical reactions that make up our life within the world. But if the religious person, when challenged by the empiricist who claims that the factual content of his faith is unprovable, were to reply that the empirical world is also essentially unprovable, its existence being equally a matter of faith — that religious person would be misunderstanding himself. It is not sufficient for the fact of salvation to be an "idea"; it would not fulfill its service to man even if, as in the case of the empirical world, its absolute reality were completely different or did not exist at all. If Jesus is not completely real, in the sense that no epistemological reservations weaken his realness, then he simply cannot have redeemed us: the reality of salvation does not permit any compromise. Certain distinguished intellectual circles today, which essentially take the position described at the beginning of this essay, fail to grasp this concrete reality of the factual content of faith, which has determined what this faith has accomplished in all the religions. With their mistaken attitude, such intellectuals are playing mythical-romantic games with the idea of God, with the transcendent significance of Jesus and with immortality. They take their justification from atavistic impulses, echoes of a vast tradition from which the crucial element, the absolute reality of the transcendent, has departed — a coquettish semiveiling of unbelief in faith itself.

Leaving aside those who have the courage neither of belief nor of unbelief in the factual content of religion, we are left with the perplexing situation of contemporary man, as described above: on the one hand, the existence of certain facts of faith to which his own intellectual conscience does not permit him access, and, on the other, the claim by outstanding thinkers of supreme intellectual power that these facts of faith are real beyond all possible doubt. He must have the troublesome feeling that he lacks a dimension of sensory perception by which others perceive something real where he could swear there is and can be nothing.

Thus he is in the threatening position of losing faith either in his own reason (by no means only in the sense of scientific evidence) or in the greatest men of history. One firm reality remains for him, however: the indubitable existence of a religious need, or, to express it more cautiously, the need that has been fulfilled by religion until now. For the Enlightenment would be utter blindness if it were to assume that with a few centuries of criticism of the content of religion, it could destroy a yearning that has dominated humanity from the first stirrings of its history, from the most primitive indigenous people to the supreme heights of culture. Yet this very point illustrates the whole predicament in which an enormous proportion of civilized humanity finds itself today: it is beset once more by powerful needs, although it sees the historical and the sole existing means of fulfilling these needs as mere fantasy, and thus is left with the needs themselves completely unanswered. Until now, religion has survived the religions as a tree survives the constant plucking of its fruit. The real gravity of the current situation is that not this or that particular dogma but the object of transcendent faith per se is characterized as illusory. What survives is no longer the form of transcendence seeking new fulfillment but something more profound and more desperate: it is a *yearning,* once fulfilled by the idea of transcendence, and now—although it is a concrete reality within the soul—paralyzed by the withdrawal of the content of faith and as if cut off from the path to its own life.

If we are to reject here any solution other than a radical reconstruction of spiritual life, we must first grasp the full meaning of the expression coined by Kant—namely, that religion is an attitude of the soul, as opposed to the vague idea that it is some mediation or mixture of spiritual being, doing, or feeling and some existence beyond this spiritual sphere. Although a relationship may exist between the soul and the transcendent, religion is surely the part of this relationship that occurs within the soul. Just as material things do not "stray into our imagination," as Kant puts it, God does not stray into our hearts. And if the claim is nonetheless made that there is a oneness or fusion of the soul with God, this claim may be assigned to the field of metaphysics or mysticism. If religion is to have a significance clearly distinct from speculation, however, it is surely a state of being or happening within the part of the soul that belongs to *us*. Somebody of an erotic nature eventually might consistently love only one other person, but his character still would have been intrinsically erotic before and independently of this individual expression of love. In the same way, a person who is religious by nature has certain inherent characteristics. By his very nature he experiences and shapes life differently from an irreligious person and would do so even if he lived on a desert island where no talk or concept of God could ever reach him.

For the sake of simplicity, I start by merely referring at first to this "religious person" in the most perfect sense. In this sense, such a person not only *has* religion as a possession or an ability. His very *being* is religious; he functions in a religious way, so to speak, just as the human body functions organically. This state of being not only adopts religious dogma as its mere *content,* realized in various forms; it also adopts the specifiably detailed qualities of the soul: the feelings of dependence and hopefulness, humility and yearning, indifference to mortality and the constraints of life. All this is still not what is profoundly religious about a religious person but is a result of his nature, something he *has.* Similarly the artist *has* imagination and technical skill, precise sensory perception, and mastery of style, whereas the substance of his being that makes him an artist is a oneness that cannot be broken down into specific features, the foundation of all else. Traditional views seem to regard religiosity as always contributing to a combination and modification of "general" spiritual energies, such as feeling, thinking, and moral or covetous desire. In reality, however, religiousness is the fundamental quality of being of the religious soul, and determines the tone and function of all these general or particular qualities of the soul. Not until afterward—though not in the temporal meaning of the word—does this fundamentally religious state of being separate into need and fulfillment, just as an artist's intrinsic character is viewed as a correlation between the creative urge and the objective creation of a work of art.

This analytical separation into *need* and *fulfillment* thus corresponds to religiousness as the nature of the religious person, on the one hand, and the objectivity of the subject matter of religion, on the other. When the timeless religious nature of an individual enters the psychological stage of need, yearning, and desire, it requires a reality as its fulfillment. This is where all those spiritual agents have their place that always have been seen as the "creators" of gods: fear and distress, love and dependence, the desire for well-being on earth and eternal salvation. Yet the whole question of the origin of religion clearly is raised only after the inner state of religiousness has been assigned this differentiated form of need and fulfillment and thus is directed toward a reality, a God that the person can believe in and commit himself to. Thus only at this stage is the question of the truth or falseness of religion raised. Clearly, this is a meaningless question if one considers religion a fundamental quality of man's nature, for only the belief in a reality beyond the believer can be true or false; a state of being cannot be. The fact that the knowledgelike element of the statement "I believe in God" is both too much and too little simply shows that the whole idea of a believing subject and a believed-in object is only a secondary analysis; it is a form of expression that does not fully reflect the deeper meaning that this is a state of being with a certain inner certitude, though alien to knowledge itself. The mystics' tentative descriptions of God as being "pure nothingness" (in contrast to any specifiable, individual thing) or as being "above" existence itself merely evade the question of God's reality, for this question is no longer on the level at which the roots of religion, or religion as the ultimate root of being itself, originates. Yet man is a creature of need; the primary direction of his being is a desire to have, and that of his subject is therefore objectivity. Hence this religious process of life, this profound disposition of the individual, is at the same time a relationship between a person of faith and a distinct object of faith and between a desirer and a provider. This form of reality thus imposes itself on religiosity itself: prayer, magic, and rite become genuinely effective instruments. When the subjective person is thus confronted with the objective reality of God, the whole question of "truth," the dispute about authenticity or illusion arises. The religious state of being, having transposed itself to this level, is split in two.

The result of this transposition, which history shows us to have been inevitable for humanity up to the present, is the emergence of "enlightenment." Its conclusion is as follows: either there is "in reality" a metaphysical, transcendental, divine sphere or being beyond mankind; or, if the scientific mind does not permit such a reality, to have faith in it one must regard it as subjective fantasy requiring psychological explanation. If this alternative presumes to be able to refute the metaphysical, the psychologically inexplicable, it is mistaken. For there is a third view: perhaps this faith, this fact of spiritual nature, is itself a metaphysical phenomenon, alive and expressing itself within this quality of being, this state of religiousness whose meaning and existence are quite independent of the content to which faith attaches itself or which it creates. When man looks up to a metaphysical-divine being, beyond all empirical detail, he is not only and always merely projecting his psychological emotions of fear and hope, exuberance and the need for redemption; he is also projecting that which is metaphysical within himself, those elements of his being that are beyond the empirical. Just as the interplay of all the rationally explicable elements of the world is based on the irreducible fact that world exists and possesses a particular origin, so the whole essentially explicable complex of psychological activity that produces the specific content of religion is based on the existence and uniqueness of the psyche, which cannot be explained rationally.

Man's particular psychological configuration assumes some origin that is not itself a product of this configuration. Feuerbach's argument stops short of this point. For him, God is simply a result of man, in his oppression, extending himself out into the infinite and seeking help from the God thus created. "Religion is anthropology": with this phrase Feuerbach attempts to dismiss the transcendent, because he sees in man only the empirical flow of spiritual objects. But he should have concluded thus: the metaphysical dimension, that which transcends the individual, is contained within the religiousness of man. Of course we should reject any attempt to deify man and similarly any anthropomorphization of God; both of these constitute a forced combination of agents, which at *their own* level are bound to be *distinct* from one another. One can preempt this dualism, however, by looking as it were behind the faith of the soul, where the object of faith emerges, and by regarding the soul's quality of religiousness as an absolute, beyond this relationship and untouched by the contrast of subject with object.

To draw an analogy, it is not our mental image of space that allows us to conclude that there is a spatial reality outside the conscious mind. If Kant is right, this mental image itself is everything we call spatial reality. In the same way, subjective religiosity does not *guarantee* the existence of a metaphysical sphere beyond itself. It is the direct realization of this sphere itself; its own reality constitutes the profundity, absoluteness, and dedication that seem to be absent from the *objects* of religious faith. This might be compared with ethics, in which moral significance is assigned not to a particular deed but to "goodwill"; "goodness" is the fundamental, indivisible character of a process of volition. Although it determines the choice of its aims, it is not these aims that are "good" and that confer the quality of goodness on the will that adopts them. On the contrary, it is the will—the spontaneous creative power of our inner being—that gives these aims their moral value. As we know, they do not display this value outwardly in their observable form. Similarly, an object of religious faith does not outwardly display its religious quality: the idea of God can be created by mere speculation, even by belief; dogmas may be the result of mere influence; the idea of salvation may simply be a result of the desire for happiness. Only through this particular quality of being that we call religious does all of this become religious itself. Just as a person's "goodwill" retains its full moral value even if fate precludes all possibilities of the person's fulfilling any actions that reflect this goodwill, so the soul retains its religious quality even if, intellectually or otherwise, the objects have been negated on which this quality of being was projected and which thus invested them with their religious character.

The religious mode of existence, however, is not simply a static, tranquil state, a *qualitas occulta,* a symbolic once-and-for-all like the beauty of some natural phenomenon or a work of art. It is a form of life in all its vitality, a way in which life vibrates, expresses itself, and fulfills its destinies. When the religious person, man as a religious being, works or enjoys himself, hopes or fears, is happy or sad—all this has a timbre and a rhythm, a relationship of the specific to the whole, an apportionment of emphasis between importance and indifference, a particular quality that is quite distinct from the same emotional experiences in a practical, artistic, or theoretical person. The major error of earlier theories of the psychology of religion, it seems to me, is that they define religiosity as the extension of such emotional experience into substantial transcendence, the creating of a God external to this experience. According to this view, faith in God is a consequence, an augmentation, a hypostatization of these purely empirical emotional experiences; life takes on a religious character only when this faith then influences life. On the contrary, I am sure that the inner spiritual processes of people who can be considered at all religious can occur only as religious in the first place, just as the movements of a graceful person are graceful in themselves. They take this quality from their source, as it were, and do not simply add it later to an essentially colorless or otherwise characterized style of movement.

Only this secondary abstraction can, within religious life, separate religion from life—though this abstraction is encouraged by the development of specific forms through which religiousness has distilled itself from the rest of life, so to speak, and constructed its own clearly delineated sphere: the transcendental world, church dogma, the doctrine of salvation. Insofar as religiosity is monopolized for this pure culture, it can separate itself from life. Rather than being a form of experience and active involvement for all aspects of life, it is one particular aspect of life among others. For this reason, for people who are only inadequately religious or not at all religious, religious dogma is the only possible way of leading some kind of religious existence. Religiousness in this case does not determine their development as its intrinsic form; therefore, they require something transcendental to look up to. For such people, religion is thus a factual and temporal affair, one might even say physically localized: the caricature of this separation of religiousness from life is its confinement to the Sunday church service. All of this can happen only if religion is a part of the content of life rather than a life itself, and if its processual nature, its pervading of the whole of life, has been transposed into a transcendental substance, somehow a separate reality — even for those truly religious individuals for whom religion is "life itself." In this way, such people have made religion into something in which it is possible to participate even if one's whole life is not determined by religion. For the truly religious, of course, religion still remains the form of all thought and action, all feeling and desire, all hope and desperation. It is not simply an added accompaniment to all this but remains the original source of all the harmonies and disharmonies of life in all their tension and release. It does not borrow its metaphysical significance from the object of its endeavor but carries it within its own being.

At this point, let us reconsider the fundamental problem addressed in these pages: how the undiminished need for religious values can achieve a sense of fulfillment if none of the specific facts of faith that previously provided this fulfillment are capable of doing so any longer. One begins to conceive of the possibility that religion will move away from its substantiality and its intrinsic bond with some transcendental content and will regain or develop an inner form or function of life itself and in all *its* aspects. The whole question here is whether the religious person can see life itself as having a metaphysical value—this life of such dedication and tension, peace and profundity, contentment and strife—and whether he is thus able, as if by a rotation of the axis, so to speak, to substitute this metaphysical value of life itself for the transcendental substance of religion. There is a profound difference between this and the words of Schleiermacher, which spring to mind here: one should not make anything out of religion, but one should do everything with it. If all aspects of life are to be lived "with religion," then religion still is something external to life, truly bonded permanently only to all thought, action, and feeling. These things, however, can exist essentially without religion, without being modified in their fundamental form. Yet a rationalistic person, for example, does not merely accompany his emotional experience and desire "with" rational reflection; rationality in fact determines the nature of his spiritual life as its all-embracing impulse. In the same way, the problem of religion today would be solved if people were to lead religious lives: not lives which are lived "with" religion, but which are religious in their very essence and which certainly are not "derived" from religion—that is, out of consideration for some object external to religious life.

However much such an object is the product of religious spiritual processes, it is nonetheless open as such to criticism. As I mentioned before, however, a state of being that is religious of itself is as exempt from criticism as any state of being, in contrast to the specific details of faith and knowledge with which it is associated: those can be subject to criticism. This indeed is the crucial problem facing all religious people: if the objects of religious yearning—not only in the historical sense, but "objects" generally—were no longer able to offer fulfillment to this desire, whether in a reactionary or a modernized form, would the religiousness of their whole being still be required to give them the sense that the meaning of their life had been profoundly fulfilled, and that the metaphysical quantum, so to speak, no longer nourished by a transcendental object, had returned to them as the meaning of existence itself? Such a rejection of all dogma— by no means in a spiteful sense—has absolutely nothing to do with religious "liberalism," for even the latter confines the religious person to specific objects, merely permitting freedom of choice between them.

The possibility that religion will develop along these lines is hampered by the fact that it seems to offer access only to those who are specifically religious by nature. But it is precisely this kind of person who will not, in any deeper sense, be at risk in this situation. Such a person may go through the doubt, the uncertain longings, the dispute, and the decline; but ultimately he will remain sure of his religion, for it is the same to him as being sure of *himself.* He finds so great a depth of being in his own consciousness that he has no need to call it God; this is why some of the most profound religious mystics display a remarkable indifference to the factual content of faith. Yet if the religious person is passionately devoted to the specifiable object of his faith, then the critical negation of its "truth," which he may not be able to avoid, will result in his adopting a different object; or else sheer desperation or iconoclastic fanaticism will lead to rejection and protest, in which religiosity has the same vital energy as before but with a negative character. A religious person is never left with nothing, for he has a fullness of being. Thus it is not he who will be faced with the difficulties that are affecting religion in the modern world; of this I have no doubt. Those who will encounter a problem here are people with only some religious elements in their nature, people who *need* religion because it is not characteristic of their being, and for whom religion fills a painfully felt gap in their existence.

The fact that it is precisely the nonreligious people who are most in need of religion, in the historical sense of faith in a transcendental reality, is less paradoxical if one takes as an analogy the fact that the completely and instinctively moral soul has no need of a separate, fixed moral code which confronts it as an imperative. It is only the temptable, the impure, the hesitant or the failing person, in whom moral consciousness—somehow imposing itself on him—becomes separated into the dictates of conscience, whereas in the wholly moral person it is an indivisible part of his being. Expressed in a traditional religious form, one could say that he who does not have God within himself needs God outside himself. The outstanding individuals of the historical religions had God both within and outside themselves. The most brilliant and most creative personalities of this kind had so powerful and so broad a sense of religion that this impulse was not exhausted by their moulding and shaping life itself. This form of life extended beyond all possible content of empirical existence to a higher plane of existence. The religious state of being could not bear its fullness and passion itself but projected itself out into the infinite and was reflected back from there, for it did not presume to be the cause or origin of its own breadth and depth, its bliss and desperation.

Yet the great majority of people simply find themselves confronted with the deity. It faces them as an objective reality that, in most cases, probably arouses the latent or semiactive religious energies within them to become real and effective. If truly religious people were to be robbed of their God through rational criticism, they would retain within them not only the source from which He originated, but also the metaphysical value that He represented. The majority of people, however, will lose everything when they lose God; for the mass needs something "objective" in quite a different sense from the intense, creative individual. The enormous question mark of the present-day situation and its future is whether the religiosity of the *average person* will succeed in turning away from the substance of God and Heaven and the transcendental "facts": in making the change to the religious shaping of life itself, and to the spiritual reality that, in philosophical terms, one could call the self-consciousness of the metaphysical significance of our existence—the change by which all otherworldly yearning and dedication, bliss and rejection, justice and mercy, are no longer found in the lofty heights above life, as it were, but in the depths within it. What is the use, in the long run, of encapsulating the realities of historical faith and attempting to preserve them in this way?

The attempt is made by means of Kantian moralizing, using ethical imperatives to artificially construct the security of a religious faith, though the latter in fact is totally different in nature. The attempt is made by means of mysticism, veiling the object of religion in such obscurity that proof of its nonexistence is impossible, with this impossibility instantly taken as proof of its existence. Attempts are made by means of Catholicism, forcing its enormous organization between the individual and its doctrine of salvation, so that the latter is a part of the concrete reality of the Church itself, and the Church therefore the only permissible means of access to such salvation; thus the individual is not held responsible for what he accepts as true. And yet it seems that the rational mind will follow a path that takes it beyond all these means and mediations by subjecting the contents of its faith to the undiluted, concrete question of being or not being. There can be no doubt about the answer in respect to the historical religions—indeed, to any religion—provided they agree on the principle of a transcendental divinity distinct from the world itself. Yet because it is equally certain that the energies which caused the growth of these manifestations of religion will not be drawn into the transience of those manifestations, it seems that the fate of religion is approaching radical change. Such change might offer these energies a different form of activity and utilization, so to speak, from that of creating transcendent images and of relating to such images. In this way, it may be that the religiousness of the soul regains the metaphysical value that the soul previously projected onto transcendent objects and that lives in those objects as the soul's life.

The mood within contemporary religiosity seems to me to invite the same interpretation as my observation over the last decade or two — that no small number of intellectually advanced individuals satisfy their religious needs by means of mysticism. On the whole, it can be assumed that these people grew up surrounded by the perspectives of one or another of the existing churches. Their turning to mysticism is unmistakably motivated by two factors. On the one hand, the forms that bind religious life to an objectively defined series of images no longer satisfy this life. On the other hand, religious yearning itself has not been deadened but seeks different goals and paths. The main reason for this yearning to be diverted towards mysticism seems to be that the latter allows the fixed definition and delimitation of religious forms to be suspended. Here, there is a deity which transcends every personalized — and thus ultimately particularized — image; it seeks an undetermined expanse of religious feeling that does not conflict with any dogmatic barrier, a deepening into formless infinity, developing only from the powerful longing of the soul. Mysticism appears to be the last refuge for

*Note:* The original text of the lecture extends from page 5 to page 48 of a self-contained publication. On pages 5 to 37, not included here, Simmel describes as a process of normal cultural change how life periodically seeks new forms with which to replace old ones. He sees it as characteristic of the modern age, however, that such forms no longer are replaced, but in many cultural domains are given up altogether as an experiment. Simmel illustrates this phenomenon with the examples of abstract art (futurist or expressionist), the craving for originality among young people, American pragmatism, and the "new ethics" as a "critique of existing sexual conditions." His final example, printed here, is that of religion.

religious individuals who cannot free themselves from all transcendental forms, but only, as it were temporarily, from those which are determined and fixed in content.

However, the most marked development—even though it may be contradictory and remain eternally remote from its goal—is that the fixed content of religious belief tends to dissolve into modes of religious life, into religiosity as the purely functional tuning of the inner process of life from which the content originally developed and still continues to develop. Until now, changes in religious culture proceeded in the way repeatedly described here: a certain outward expression of religious energy, originally fully appropriate to that energy in its strengths and inherent characteristics, gradually stiffens into superficialities and narrowness. It is then displaced by a newly arising form in which the dynamism and urgency of the religious impulse finds immediate expression; in other words, it is still a religion, a series of beliefs, that is taking the place of an outmoded one.

For a very large number of people today, however, the supernatural objects of religious belief have been excised radically, though without these people's religious impulse having been eliminated as a result. The energy within this impulse, however, which formerly manifested itself in the discovery of new, more satisfying dogmatic content, no longer feels it can articulate itself in the polarity of a believing subject and a believed object. In the ultimate condition that this inner discord anticipates, religion would occur as a way of living life itself. It would be analogous not to a single melody in the symphony of life, but to the key in which the whole work is performed. The space of life, filled entirely by the content, actions and fate, thoughts and feelings of the world, would be permeated with that unique inner unity between humility and assertiveness, tension and peace, danger and consecration, which can only be called religious. A person living life in this fashion would have an inherent sense of the absolute value of such a life—a value which otherwise seemed to be given to it only through the specific forms in which it was contained and through the specific content of belief toward which it had crystallized. Angelus Silesius gives us a foretaste of this, albeit transposed into the last remaining form available to mysticism, when he separates religious value from all fixed connections with anything specific and recognizes its place as lived life:

> The saint when he is drinking
> Is just as pleasing to God
> As if he were praying and singing.

What we are dealing with here is not so-called secular religion. The latter still clings to determinate content, though in this case it is empirical rather than transcendental; secular religion also channels religious life into specific forms of beauty and greatness, sublimity and lyrical motion — in fact, it feeds on the hidden but still effective remnants of transcendental religiosity, an obscure hybrid. Mysticism, however, raises the question of whether religiosity is a direct process of life, encompassing every pulse beat. Mysticism is a "being," not a "having," a type of piety that would be called faith if it had objects, but which is in fact a way in which life itself is lived. It does not aim to satisfy needs deriving from some external source — just as an expressionistic painter does not satisfy his artistic needs by clinging to an exterior subject — but instead searches for continuous life at a depth where such life has not yet become split into needs and their fulfillment and therefore does not require some "object" to impose a specific form on it. Such life wishes to express itself directly as religious, not through a language with a given vocabulary and a prescribed syntax. It would only seem to be a paradox to state: "The soul wants to keep its quality of faith, although it has lost faith in all determined and predefined religious content."

This orientation of religious souls can often be sensed in attempts at a purely negative criticism, strangely lacking in clarity and betraying a misunderstanding of their own position. And indeed, such mysticism encounters the most profound difficulty of all: life can express itself in the sphere of the mind only by means of forms in which its own freedom can become a reality, although at the same time such forms set limits to this freedom. Piety, or the quality of faith, is certainly a disposition of the soul, an integral part of its life; it colors the soul even in the permanent absence of a religious object, just as an erotic individual would conserve and benefit from his erotic qualities even though he might never meet a lovable person. Nevertheless, I wonder whether the fundamental will of religious life does not inevitably require an object. Surely this merely functional character of religiosity is in fact a formless energy which can confer upon the ups and downs of life only a certain coloring and grandeur. While it appears to represent the definitive meaning of so much religious feeling, perhaps it is no more than an intermediate phenomenon that remains purely conceptual, the outward expression of a situation in which religious inner life breaks through and rejects the existing forms of religion without the ability to replace them with new ones. And of course here as well as elsewhere the idea arises that life could make do without any forms of objective significance or demands and could simply survive with its own vitality, erupting from within. One of the most profound emotional difficulties of countless people in the modern world is that it is impossible for them to continue to maintain the religions that are based on church tradition, while the religious urge itself persists despite all "enlightenment" (after all, such enlightenment can rob religion only of its clothing, not of its life). There is a tempting way out of this dilemma in the cultivation of religious life to become something entirely self-sufficient, in the transformation of religious faith from a transitive to an intransitive activity, as it were, though this solution might eventually become equally entangled in contradictions.

In all of this and in other phenomena we see the conflict that life by its very nature confronts whenever it is cultural in the broadest sense of the term, in other words when it is creative or acquires that which has been created. Such life must either produce forms or proceed through forms. We *are* life in its immediacy—and equally immediately associated with this fact is a feeling of being, energy, and direction that cannot be specified more clearly—but we *have* life only as expressed in forms of whatever kind, which, as I have emphasized above, belong to a completely different order as soon as they come into being; these forms are endowed with rights and meanings of independent provenance, and they claim and assert a status that is entirely their own. This, however, brings about a contradiction with the essence of life itself, with its undulating dynamics, its temporal destinies, the unceasing differentiation of all its components. Life can enter reality only in the form of its counterimage—that is, only as a *form*. This contradiction becomes more urgent and appears more irreconcilable as this emotional reality—which we can only call life—makes itself increasingly felt in its formless strength,[1] and to the extent that such forms present themselves in this rigidly individual status, claiming their inalienable rights as the true meaning or value of our existence. This tendency seems to have increased as culture has evolved.

Here, life wishes to obtain something that it cannot reach. It desires to transcend all forms, determining itself and appearing in its naked immediacy. Yet the processes of thinking, wishing, and shaping can only substitute one form for another; life can never replace form as such, because life transcends form. All

---

[1] Because life is the antithesis of form, and because only that which is formed somehow can be described conceptually, the concept of life cannot be freed from logical imprecision. The essence of life would be denied if one tried to form a conceptual definition of it. Only as a life that is conscious of itself in its own motion, life is in the position of bypassing the conceptual level that coincides with the realm of forms. That the possibilities of expression are so limited by the essence of life does not diminish the clarity of this fundamental antagonism [footnote by Simmel].

these attacks—whether passionately aggressive or slowly progressive—against the forms of our culture are in fact either an overt or a covert assault on the power of life itself—as life and because it is life; they embody the deepest internal contradictions of the mind as soon as it presents itself as culture—that is to say, in forms. And it seems to me that although this chronic conflict has become acute in many historical eras and has sought to pervade the whole of human existence, no other era but ours has revealed it so clearly as its motivating force.

It is, however, narrow-minded prejudice to believe that conflicts and problems exist merely for the sake of being solved. In fact, both have other functions in the processes and history of life, functions they fulfill independently of their solutions. Thus in no sense are they lost causes, even if the future does not replace conflicts with their resolutions but only replaces their forms and contents with others. For of course all the problems that have been mentioned bring to mind that the present is far too contradictory to allow us to stay with it. In the degree of its contradictoriness, it undoubtedly points to a more fundamental change than would occur if it were simply a matter of changing an existing form into an emerging one. If the latter is the case, the bridge between "before" and "after" hardly ever seems to have been torn down so completely in the past as now, when nothing but formless life itself appears to step into the breach. With equal certainty, however, we are moving toward a typical cultural change, the creation of new forms adapted to contemporary forces—though these new forms will still only replace one problem with another, one conflict with another, even if general awareness is slower to develop and open battle is postponed for longer. But in this way the true essence of life is fulfilled: a battle in the absolute sense, encompassing the relative polarity of war and peace, while absolute peace, which might encompass both these poles equally, remains a divine secret.

**PART 2** *Religion and Personality*

One of the great intellectual achievements of religion is that it draws together the vast spectrum of human ideas and concerns and concentrates them into single, unified concepts; unlike those of philosophy, these concepts are not abstract but rather possess the full vitality of being themselves in their immediacy and inner tangibility. God—the highest reality, ultimate source, and estuary of all currents of individual being, above and in all things at the same time, that which is most common to all and yet the unique and most personal possession of every soul. Sanctification—the ultimate perfection of any moral endeavor, beyond attainment through individual actions and yet not a pale abstraction like so many purely moral ideals but rather arousing the soul in all its passion, like a call exhorting the prisoner to break his chains. Eternal life—the unification and fulfillment of all the values and energies of our fragmentary existence; not a conceptual scheme such as Plato's world of ideas, but something intimately connected with our most personal being and—whether it is the hunting grounds of the American Indian afterlife or the walls of eternal Zion—radiant in the clarity of the most unerring truth.

The salvation of the soul belongs in the same category as these concepts but is to be distinguished from both the soul's sanctification and its immortality. For we speak of the soul's salvation as signifying the satisfaction of all its ultimate longing, by no means merely in moral terms but also in terms of its yearning for transcendence and fulfillment, stature and strength. In fact, we do not mean any specifiable good from which might emanate the fulfillment of these longings; instead, the very essence of the concept is that it denotes the point at which all these strivings and energies come together and become one. It is not something toward which we might direct our longings; rather, it describes their position.

It also signifies something of a supremely spiritual quality. Thus to ask whether a soul that has found salvation is in a mortal body or in some heavenly domain is utterly superfluous and in-consequential—as inconsequential as if one wished to know in which house one was to meet one's fate. By salvation of the soul we mean the ultimate unity of all its innermost perfections, on which it can agree only with itself and with its God. This is not the unity of a concept, but the unity of a state that we can feel although we have not attained it, or, perhaps better, a state that is as real to us when we long for it as it would be when fulfilled within us.

Among the innumerable forms that this ideal can assume, Christian teaching occasionally refers to one that seems to me especially noteworthy. When a person achieves his very best and fulfills everything of which he is capable according to his own ideals, or, in religious terms, if he fulfills all that God has demanded of him and has promised him—if this is the case, we often feel that this person has developed or realized some-thing outwardly that in fact was already inherent in him. We feel that part of the truth of this person's nature, which had thus far simply not yet been perceptible, so to speak, has now taken on this new form. According to this view—which admittedly is only suggested occasionally, alongside directly opposing views —the soul's fulfillment does not mean that it gains something new, not even in the sense that the ripened fruit is something new in comparison with the mere seed. Instead every person has within him the ideal of his own self—potentially, but in reality, too. The self's pure form, what it ought to be, is an ideal reality that pervades the imperfect reality of existence; thus it is merely a question of "casting off the old Adam" and revealing the per-fect being beneath it, of "crucifying the flesh" to free that better part of us which is already there within us.

When the angels carry Faust's immortal soul to salvation

and initially receive him like a butterfly's pupa, they sing, "Loosen the flakes that surround him—see how the holy life invests him with beauty and grandeur." The inner core need only be freed from that which masks and restrains it. This is the very essence of the soul's salvation: nothing needs to be added or affixed to it from outside, but it really needs only to cast off a shell and fulfill its inner being. How otherwise should we interpret the notion of having been created God's children, if this did not mean the inheritance of ultimate perfection—not a perfection that we have yet to acquire, but one that we have only to reflect on and to bring out of ourselves, as it were?

Of course, our lives, and especially our practical application of morality, demand active involvement of us, *creating* new forms and contents. But if we inquire as to the meaning of all this activity to our innermost soul, it seems—inasmuch as this activity is good and holy—that we are only revealing the real core of our being, which was already there, so that we can see ourselves in radiant clarity, where sin and error previously had made us unrecognizable, blurring our true contours with dim shadows. Everything outside the soul that has power over it must first be discarded. When this has been done, the soul will already have found its salvation: for in doing so, it will have found itself: "He who loses his soul shall gain it!"

At the same time, all selfishness is cast off as well, for selfishness is always a relationship between the soul and that which is extraneous to it. The soul expects some gain from outside, some happiness, for which it exploits its surroundings. Any selfishness is a mixing of the soul with extrinsic elements, a mistaken path on which the soul errs, a desire of the soul to fill a gap in itself that it cannot fill on its own. The soul that has achieved complete and absolute self-fulfillment, however, has no need of this. Nothing extraneous to it can arouse longing or selfishness within it, because it always has itself and is nothing but the culmination of its innermost being. It is thus both longing and fulfillment at one and the same time.

This explains the sensation of freedom we experience in all actions that we know to be paving the way to our soul's salvation. Man is free to the extent that the center of his being determines its periphery—that is, when our individual thoughts and decisions, our actions and our suffering alike, are an expression of our real self, undiverted by forces that do not form part of us. An action is not free if it hovers indeterminately, but only if it carries the bold stamp of the very core of our personality in all its strength and coloring.

It is peculiar to the ideal of the soul's salvation as suggested in the Christian faith—albeit in fragmentary fashion—that this carving out of our personality, its liberation from all that is not itself, this realization of the conception and law of the self, is the same as being obedient to *God's* will, living according to *His* principles, and that it is in harmony with the ultimate values of being itself. The salvation sought after by the soul would not be its *own,* but a colorless and spiritually alien one, if the path toward it were not mapped out already within the soul itself, and if it were not gained through a process of discovery of the self. But for this very reason there are a great many concepts of salvation that, as it were, force themselves on the soul, like some extraneous, alien force imposing a transformation on it. This kind of salvation, dependent as it is on practical actions or dogmatic belief, is to the soul itself fortuitous, and thus is a blind compulsion that destroys its freedom. Only if the substance of religious demands made on an individual is real within himself and need only be freed from that which is not himself—only then can the sphere of religious salvation be equated with the realm of freedom.

This point is illustrated especially clearly when contrasted with Judaism before the prophets. In this case there is a sharp distinction between the self and the divine principle: not only when Jehovah appears as an Oriental despot whose will in itself is law and to whom the Jewish people look up in servitude, but also when the relationship between the two is expressed as a covenant granting each party inalienable rights. In both cases the Law is something extraneous to the individual, and for this reason the reward for its fulfillment also consists of something extraneous: his well-being on earth. Here are precisely those conditions of selfishness described above. Salvation is not achieved by realizing the soul's innermost nature, for which there can be no greed. It is gained by wresting as much power as possible from the soul's surroundings, whether by obedience, deception, or force. And this very dependence of the way of life on extraneous elements prevents life from being set free. A mentality of servitude remains, thus laying bare the full extent of the common root of selfishness and unfreedom. The Law must set a reward for its fulfillment because its substance is not something that is within the self or connected with it intrinsically; on the contrary, the Law erects a barrier to the self. It is not an extension and an enhancement of the empirical individual emanating from the self's inner ideal but imposes itself as a constraint in the predominantly prohibitive form of "thou shalt not."

This interpretation of the soul's salvation as the deliverance, the demystification, so to speak, of the soul's essence, an essence that is always present but is mixed with alien, impure, and fortuitous elements — such an interpretation seems to clash with one particular basic precept of Christianity: the equal ability of *every* individual to achieve ultimate salvation, the fact that this salvation depends on accomplishments that from the very outset are not inaccessible to anyone. There is room for everyone in God's house because the greatest that can be achieved by any human is, at the same time, the least that is to be expected of him, and therefore in principle cannot be withheld from anybody. But if salvation is to consist of nothing but that each and every soul should express and become totally immersed in its innermost being, the pure image of itself whose contours are imposed as an ideal form on its mortal imperfection — how, then, is it possible to reconcile the infinite variety of souls in their stature and depth, their breadth and limitations, their brilliance and darkness, with equality of religious accomplishment and equal worthiness before God? How indeed, since this concept of salvation singles out as its very vehicle those elements of a person's being which are most individual and which distinguish him most from others?

It is true that the difficulty of reconciling equality before God with the immeasurable diversity of individuals has led to that uniformity of religious achievement which has turned much of Christian life into mere schematism. Christians have failed to take account of all the individualism inherent in the Christian concept of salvation, the idea that each person should make the most of *his own talent;* they have been demanding of everyone a single, uniform goal and identical behavior instead of asking every person simply to give of himself. Anything that is globally uniform must remain superficial to an individual's personality. That oneness which unites the faithful, the equality of perfect souls, consists only of each individual's outward actions being permeated with the inner essence that is peculiar to himself; the actual substances of individual essences may be worlds apart. Jesus indicates in a number of instances how much he values the diversity of individual potential within human beings but at the same time how little this affects the equality of the final outcome of life. Thus the crux here is the extent to which this ideal of the self, already mapped out within each person, is allowed to penetrate into a person's empirical reality.

There is no mistaking one thing, however: the more the soul's salvation is based on its individuality, possibly beyond comparison with any other, the less the person will be able to find respite from having to concentrate on what is most personal and unique within the individual. The more perilous life is, the more exposed the individual's spiritual conviction, the more complete is his responsibility for his own self. This is why Nietzsche totally misunderstands Christianity when he regards it as a kind of insurance policy for the masses. The fact that one must engage in a battle of self-assertion against one's self in order to achieve salvation means that a terrible inner danger exists, something that is reflected outwardly in the doctrine of election. Everything hangs on the central concern; there is no universal solution for its accomplishment, but rather a unique route for each individual—even if the religious goal to which all individual routes lead is one and the same.

Where Christianity approaches this concept of salvation, it touches on the most deeply rooted problem of the contemporary world. For whether in morality or in art, in social life or in the principles of knowledge, we seek the universally valid that also is applicable in specific cases, laws that relate both to the individual and to all people, and the universal model that embraces the unique and the particular. Until now, either one or the other has been held up as the norm; yet all of our contemporary dilemmas depend on a synthesis of the two.

The salvation of the soul, that most far-reaching and most universal of challenges to all humanity, depends on each and every person's wresting from himself the most personal and unique elements of his being, real in conception but not yet pure in form. If this is so, this concept might reveal itself as one of the motivating forces behind an instinctive and tentative rediscovery of religion in the modern world—as if the most deeply rooted concerns and afflictions of our lives were to find in religion if not a solution, at least a form of expression and the consolation of knowing that our difficulties today are the same as those which have always confronted humanity.

*Coincidentia oppositorum*—the coincidence of opposites, the unification of that which has been torn asunder. Such is the definition of God given by Nicolaus Cusanus, the most searching philosopher of the fifteenth century, a precursor of Copernicus and of modern individualism, too, in that his teachings stressed the uniqueness of all things and that each entity, in its incomparability, represents in its place the universe. The cause of the world's infinite diversity, however, is contained within God's own oneness, which cannot be proved in terms of logic and reason, but which requires no proof because it is only the reflection of an emotional relationship of the soul with existence. The essence of all mysticism is that we should perceive behind the given multiplicity of phenomena that unity of being which is never a given fact, and which therefore we can grasp directly only within ourselves as this unity. All mysticism is a fusion of the self with the deity, for there is no other way of channeling the unbearable multiplicity and unfamiliarity of all things into one, except through our soul.

This unifying of the fragments and contradictions of our view of the world by attributing to them one common, all-embracing source may be the earlier achievement of religion, historically speaking, but it is perhaps only of secondary importance. Of more fundamental significance, especially as far as modern man is concerned, is what religion makes of the contradictions of spiritual life. Just as this theistic or pantheistic mysticism reconciles the fragmentary nature of the world's elements by unifying them in God, so religious behavior brings peace to the opposing and incompatible forces at work within the soul, resolving the contradictions they create. The subjective significance of religion to the soul is thus a reflection of what God as the object of religion does for our worldview.

Just as it is a childish superstition to think that one can recognize God in any specific feature of the world, and just as a supramundane power can be inferred only far beyond all these single features in the integration of the whole, so all religiousness is one-sided and dependent on the fortuities of individual fate if it is based on a single emotion: humility or elevation, hope or remorse, despair or love, passion or calm. For however much one of these emotions may ultimately dominate, the essence of religiousness is that it creates equal space for all these pairs of opposites. This is not to say that a sense of religion already within us arouses these emotions or harnesses them; religiousness means that these feelings now flow together like the waves of a single current, although they were aroused by the conflicting impressions of the world and our fate in it. These conflicting forces now suggest a deeper, hidden unity as if they were merely the functions of different limbs bearing the life of a single organism. The focus of religion, its spiritual center, so to speak, is fixed at the point of intersection where these rays emanate from all layers of the soul. A physical object becomes real for us by appealing to different senses simultaneously; we would not call a ghost an object if it were only visible and not tangible. It would have to be perceivable, at least potentially, by different senses; the greater the number of senses that can locate it, the more objective, definitive, and fixed it becomes: thus a large number of diverse concerns of our lives must converge—indeed, their very plurality must make itself felt—in order for the focus of religion to be defined. They do not converge at a point previously fixed: this point is created by their convergence. This point of focus of our religious endeavor must be placed, of course, in a sphere beyond the empirical world, because it would be impossible to reconcile our manifold and diverse spiritual concerns in an empirical context.

Since the religious mood within us is the unifying force of

all the diverse currents of our spiritual life, just as God is for all being, the truly religious person does not view religion as the celebration of certain specific moments in his life, like the garlands of roses that enhance the day's festivities but wither in the evening. The religious mood is present, at least potentially, at every moment of that person's life, because to him it is the very foundation of life, the source of all his energies. This experience is simply a reflection of the confluence of the multitude of spiritual currents from contradictory sources on the common ground of religion. It is as if love and alienation, humility and pleasure, delight and regret, despair and trust were to confront us in bewildering disarray and disharmony in our empirical experience, but as if, by extending them beyond the mortal plane, as it were, they were all to converge at one fixed point. The specific spiritual state that we describe as religious embraces all these movements of the soul, or rather is called into being through their combination. And just as we are easily led to believe that a passion apparently fired by inexhaustible spiritual energies within us is the very source of these energies, a religious person believes that his religiousness is the source of all these conflicting emotions; whereas in fact, religion is that form peculiar to him in which all the contradictions of his soul are reconciled and united in a single focal point.

This tension and disharmony of the emotions is actually necessary in order to convey fully the unity of the object of our faith and our behavior toward it, in the sense that here, again, it is as if some resistance is needed for the power of religion to express itself and make itself felt. This tension is perhaps most strongly apparent in the affective sphere of love. Love is the name given by Plato to a condition halfway between having and not having. But love is not only beyond the superficial antithesis of having and not having, as a third condition that brings to bear the distinctiveness of its purest essence, even when it occurs in its most forthright, outward forms. Love is also a true mixture of the two. It means to have and not to have at one and the same time, an infinitely secure possession that nevertheless, each day and with untiring efforts, must be acquired anew, not merely preserved. For the possession of love carries the inherent need to be increased, and with this increase it becomes more certain that even the most unfettered mutual possession of love still leaves one ultimate unknown that has yet to be won over, as if love had one unattainable goal—whether abrogation of the self or whatever else we may wish to call it—a goal that it can approach only in the realm of the infinite. This duality takes its most distinct form in the unique contraposition of God to the person of faith. For such a person, God is the one possession of which he is surest, just as sure as he is of his own self.

For just as we often may feel that our self is the only real entity in a world that is "mere idea," a shadowy and unreal dream world, so the person of faith sees all things on this earth as a mere nothing, as bursting bubbles or dim shadows compared to the One and Only that is solid and immutable. Thus all possessions are sacrificed for it—"body, land, honor, child and wife"—because these, of course, are not really possessions but dreams and specters. There again, however, the unshakable certainty of this possession lies infinitely beyond the believer himself. Just as he who prays "Lord, teach me faith" must already have faith in God, so he who seeks to find God afresh every day, yet more deeply and more fully, must already have found him. Encompassing in a single spiritual truth the logical contradiction between desiring a possession most deeply and savoring it most fully, this most extreme stage of faith is something that every form of love emulates because the stage of desire anticipates the desired state itself. The counterpart is that every fulfilled desire contains a longing that the state of fulfillment can never quite satisfy. For this reason it is quite apt to speak of God as "Love" itself; love thus is seen to be that constellation of spiritual forces in which, for us, God is alive. In our feeling for God, the tension between having and not having reaches its ultimate climax; for whether this emotion remains finite in our love for finite beings or whether it merely hints vaguely and uncertainly at the infinite, both are directed toward Him, and therefore are truly infinite. The religious soul is bound to its God equally strongly by the bonds of having and those of not having; or rather one might say that its God comes into being at the point where these conflicting bonds, extended beyond the finite world, converge.

There is another way in which the powers of faith within us seem to span even greater contradictions in our spiritual life. They reconcile not only conflicting forces—this would almost seem to be the simpler task—but also those unrelated elements in which no truly direct antagonism exists. That part of our soul which is weighed down, as it were, by the forces of gravity, the dullness and dreariness within us, is by no means engaged in constant and direct conflict with the ideals and principles that strive to uplift this sagging life force, in the kind of conflict with which superficial moralism concerns itself. No: what is most terrible about the opposition between "the Law" and what Paul calls the flesh is that they operate at quite different levels. That which is dark, sinful, selfish, and sensual within us and that other side of our nature, striving upward as a flame and transcending mortal birth—these two often seem not to come into contact at all, as if there were a neutral zone between them, rather like the desolate area it was once customary to designate between the borders of two countries. Many situations that we encounter in our spiritual lives can be expressed only in terms of an emptiness and indifference lying between the realm of radiant perfection and the realm of despondency and oppression, an impassible barrier that prevents a direct confrontation between the two. It is one of the most profound experiences, which no metaphor can express adequately, that the very best side of our nature very often fails to find a point of departure within us, some lever with which to tear out the evil; such an evil does not even put up a positive fight but is simply there. Perhaps this is the ultimate meaning of the saying, "The spirit is willing, but the flesh is weak": the flesh does not of itself afford any point of leverage from which it might be purified and raised into the realm of the ideal. Paul seems to have had a profound sense that this contradiction is not a simple battle of opposites, but that a lack of relatedness between the two often completely precludes the victory of one over the other.

So it is that a third force is required, which transcends both, battling out the conflict of which these two are not capable. When the whole person reconciles himself to God, all the parts of his being, the Law and the flesh, also are reconciled to one another. All of those expressions which seem to add a certain materialistic crudeness to religion, such as the resurrection of the flesh and the like, are surely only imperfect attempts to dramatize the sense that God is just as much a God of reality as of the ideal. This is why religiosity also is imbued with those dark, sensual, oppressive elements of humanity, in asceticism and in ecstasy alike. Incidentally, this again explains why it is false to reduce religion to mere morals in an attempt to overcome or deny these baser elements for the benefit of the higher ideals. Religion is by no means so one-dimensional. Where religion emphasizes "reconciliation," in primitive sacrificial cultures no less than in Christianity itself, this is a spiritual truth that, quite apart from any metaphysical significance, refers to the reconciliation of the elements of man's nature. Very often only religion's sweeping inspiration of the soul allows those layers of dull passivity to become malleable for higher spiritual and ethical energies; mere morals would simply lead these energies into rigid confrontation with the passive layers.

Yet another type of antithetical pair that combines in religion, or whose combination brings religion about, might be termed the destitution and the abundance of life. There is more truth than one might expect in the idea—usually expressed ironically—that distress and affliction, both outward and inward, made man create the gods, and that prayer is something we learn only in times of trouble. No doubt many people have turned to faith reluctantly and resignedly, only when all of life's other resources have failed. This does not always mean, however, that we are seeking something we cannot find within ourselves, desiring some gain by turning to faith. Rather, it is the case that hardship and misfortune simply make the soul assume a form, as it were, in which it is especially receptive to religious sentiments. Although happiness could teach us just as well, in fact it is only in suffering that we learn fully how our existence exposes us to insuperable forces, like a mere leaf exposed to the winds. We come to know the nature of fate only in life's harshness, just as only the broken-hearted are said to know what true love is. This creates within us a space for the specifically religious feeling of being confronted with the infinite. In a person of religious disposition, the sheer amount of personal suffering leads above and beyond the individual, as if this suffering were to burst out of the insubstantial vessel of the self, leading it on into the realm of the infinite. Of course it is childish to call for God's help in particular instances of superficial need; but if a person feels distress as something emanating from the very core of his soul, as that which determines the relationship of his being to his ideals and to reality, the cry for God does not issue from the distress of an individual subject but from creation, from being itself, demanding its right to transcendence. The fortuitous individual distress that gave rise to the appeal is left behind; its sole focus becomes the ultimate goal toward which we strive.

Yet the abundance of our lives reaches out to this very same goal. Religion also pours forth from the exalted soul that cannot contain its exuberance by itself, casting it out into the infinite, so to speak, to receive it back from that realm. It is as if some absolute power beyond the soul were needed as the only possible explanation of this feeling, which the soul itself cannot comprehend. Here religion does not make up for some shortcoming within us but expresses life's supreme bliss, man's excess, a step he takes beyond himself, where he is not too small for himself, but too great. This very overflowing of life which absolutizes the individual's strength and vigor, this, too, is a source of religion, this, too, is one of the forces that are cast in the mould of religion, just like the very opposite, life's distress and destitution, perhaps experienced by the same soul.

Now we come to a final point. Religion is one of the elements of life: it must take its place among the other elements and must develop a relationship with them if life is to be an integrated whole. At the same time, religion is a counterpart to that which we would otherwise call our empirical life. It stands beside life as an equivalent power, expressing and balancing out the whole of life in its own right. Religion therefore is a limb and a whole organism at one and the same time—a part of our existence, and yet also that whole existence itself on an elevated, spiritual plane. It relates to the other elements of our lives in the most diverse and most contrasting ways; yet it is raised above life, too. Therefore, in its moments of greatest intensity, it is raised above itself in the reconciliation of all the conflicts that it entered as a single element of life. One could well express this unique form of reconciliation the other way around. Man needs religion in order to reconcile several conflicting forces: his needs and the satisfaction of these needs, what he should do and what he actually does, his ideal view of the world and reality. Religion, however, does not remain hovering above all of these as an elevated power of reconciliation but descends onto the battlefield itself; it takes sides, though it is also the judge. But it raises itself again, above the conflict thus joined, to become its own higher authority, reconciling within itself the dualism it has brought about. Thus at every moment it is unity and unity yet to be; it resolves the contradictions it finds outside itself as well as those which arise constantly between itself and the totality of the rest of life.

This is clearly an endless process. Man cannot constantly maintain the perfect oneness of life itself and that of life and religion as well. It is rather as if, again and again, the mists were to rise from the murky depths of the soul and those forces were to emerge from them, taking up the struggle among themselves and against religious life, even if this now takes place before a higher judge. Once again, some greater momentum is needed, some more profound relationship to the absolute, to quell the strife that has arisen between the newly won harmony and those elements it once more fails to contain or its powers of reconciliation. And yet this very understanding of religion as a never-ending task, as a process of development in which each stage attains points infinitely beyond itself—this will enable modern man to turn to faith once again. For it is not only his nature to demand of religion, of his subjective relationship to God, the reconciliation of opposites within his own life instead of allowing all conflicts of creation to be resolved within God. It is also important not to leave untouched and untroubled the higher reconciliatory power itself, for it must not be allowed to become rigid and fixed beyond all contradiction. This development works its way tirelessly through each new formation of conflicting forces, until it finally attains that spiritual dimension whose essence is the reconciliation of all opposites. It is at this point that the rhythm of modern life will have triumphed over the very last resistance. It also will have laid down with unmistakable clarity a task for the future: to find within those endless contradictions and turbulences the redemption and reconciliation that until now have appeared to offer only an escape from them.

Discussions about the existence of God often reach a stage at which the person affirming God's existence claims that although he is not actually able to state *what* God is, he believes or knows *that* God is. This is not the idea of the mystics, who claim that God is "nothingness"; their assertion simply reflects an unwillingness to specify some particular feature of God, a clarification which of necessity would result in something one-sided, limiting, and exclusive and thus would negate the all-embracing, omnipresent universality of the divine principle. The divine "nothingness" of the mystics expresses the idea that God is nothing specific, but that He is indeed—and for this very reason—totality itself. The first-mentioned affirmation, however, contains nothing of this pantheistic meaning; rather it contains the odd illogic of asserting the existence of a thing while at the same time not being at all capable of stating what it actually is. The critic would be justified in questioning the legitimacy of calling this something God, on the grounds that God is an empty word if the reality of the concept is asserted but not the slightest indication can be given of *what* reality the term refers to. The psychological motive for this statement might be described as follows: as far as modern man is concerned, the concept of God has passed through so much heterogeneous historical content and so many possibilities of interpretation that all that remains is a feeling that cannot be fixed in any precise form—something much more general than the abstract concept that might be the common denominator of all these various definitions of God.

One might call this the extreme of faith: the person simply believes, so to speak. Belief in its purest form is active in his soul, but the specific object or content of this faith is not definable in any way. To express this from the perspective of the object, the question or fact of *being* has won the prerogative in the logic of the religious consciousness, existence has overcome its own factual content, so to speak. This idea was first given particular emphasis by Parmenides, for whom only an all-embracing, unified being *exists,* whereas all definitions and details are inessential and insignificant. Here it is the *existence* of God that attracts all interest, and—however strange it must seem when expressed in such an abstract way—the question of *what* He is vanishes in the abyss of this notion of His existence. There is a connection between these two sides, the objective and the subjective: the object of faith is a being. What it is and how it comes to be—these are the product of rational thought, intuition, and tradition, but this product remains indefinite, a still-dubious conceptualization. It is faith that invests it with that solidity of being which the intellect and the imagination cannot encompass with their qualitative and quantitative definitions. Faith is, as it were, the sensory organ by which this being is conveyed to us.

There is a close relationship through which this being is accessible only to faith. Faith, if we are to be precise, is oriented solely toward this being, and it is as if this relationship were to mark one pole of the religiously oriented consciousness. The other pole is the accumulation of spiritual energies that make up the religious world in terms of its *content*—that is, the definitions of God's nature, the doctrine of salvation, and the imperatives of conduct. Thus we have the content of religion, on the one hand, and the faith in its reality, on the other. Even though these two poles are absolutely inseparable in the experienced reality of religious life, they are nonetheless distinct, from an analytical point of view, though not only in this way. For these two poles define the distinct positions of the religious person on the one hand, and of the philosopher of religion on the other. To the former, faith is the essential element; the content of faith is, so to speak, of secondary significance by comparison, although such a person would sacrifice his own life for the truth of this content. This point is illustrated by the fact that many deeply religious individuals are indifferent to any kind of dogma, and that the various dogmas are products of the infinite fortuities of history — whereas the religiousness of these individuals is unquestionably the same in essence, even though the content of what they believe in is so diverse. The form of religion that determines their view of reality is the same for all of them, even though the details of their beliefs might be as heterogeneous as one possibly could imagine. For the philosopher of religion, by contrast, who takes this content as the object of his theoretical construction, psychological description, or logical criticism, it is irrelevant for such purposes whether this content is believed in and whether it is true at all. Similarly, *mutatis mutandis,* the mathematician deals with geometric figures, unconcerned about whether they have counterparts in physical reality and how these figures and the laws relating to them that he has discovered might be significant for the processes of practical consciousness.

This philosophical perspective, therefore, is not subject to any religious decisions because it consists merely of an immanent evaluation of the meaning, structure, and logical status of the content of religion rather than a judgment of its reality. It is from this perspective that I will examine the concept of the "personality" of the divine principle. Perhaps no other concept in this field has aroused such vehement opposition from so many different camps. The "Enlightenment" takes it as evidence that religion is merely a deification of man himself; conversely, pantheism and mysticism view it as an anthropomorphization. There is, however, a higher perspective that avoids both of these criticisms. The immediate cause for a "personal God" in psychological terms may be that humans exist as persons; but the logical and metaphysical foundation of the concept is nevertheless quite independent of this idea.

What is the meaning of personality? It seems to me that this term describes the culmination and perfection that the physical organism gains by being extended into spiritual being. The organism is a segment of physical being whose parts interact more closely than any combination of such elements that we describe as inorganic. "Life" pursues its cycle within a closed sphere, in which all the parts determine each other in a dynamic coherence that we characterize as "unity." In this objective sense, no single inorganic element can be described as possessing "unity." A rock or a lump of metal is "one" in the numerical sense only, because it is one specimen of a term that has been applied to it; when split mechanically, each of its parts again is rock or metal, possessing unity only in the same way as did the larger piece previously. If a living being is cut into parts, however, none of these parts has the same unity as before, when it belonged to the whole. Yet the unity by which the elements of a physical organism mutually define their form and function is not complete, because the living being undergoes a constant process of exchange with its environment. This process of giving and taking shows that it is included in a larger whole, so that it cannot be regarded as a unity in the strict sense—that is, as a self-sufficient entity, completely comprehensible from the relationship of all its parts to one another. Insofar as this organism has a conscious soul, however, its contents provide a degree of interrelatedness and mutual interdependence that goes far beyond mere physical unity.

The difference here stems from a fundamental distinction between the spiritual and the physical: in the physical world, the cause disappears in its effect. Once the effect has occurred, the cause becomes entirely irrelevant, to the point that it is not possible even to deduce a cause from an effect with any certainty. This type of causality also exists in the spiritual sphere. Here, however, in addition to this causality—or rather within it—there is another causality that we call memory. Memory means that a past event is not only a cause in the physical sense, transferring its quantum of energy, its impulse, and its character into an effect that morphologically might be completely different. Rather, memory returns as a later occurrence, retaining its content and morphological identity, so to speak. As mentioned earlier, any physical effect could essentially be generated by any number of quite different causes. A recollected mental image, however, as long as it is still in active memory, can have only a single cause, namely, the substantially identical mental image that originated in the person's consciousness at some previous point in time—providing, of course, that the whole course of events between the two and the entire state of the psyche allow recollection to occur at all. This leads to a unique configuration: the passage of time, as such, leaves past occurrences in the past and allows them to have an *effect* on later events only without the later events' being able to respond and to create *interaction* between the two; memory, on the other hand, transports what is past into the present, thereby leaving it relatively unaffected by the passage of time.

Yet the elements of consciousness necessarily influence one another; that is to say, we can conceive of the continuous flux of our inner life only by means of the symbol that the contents of life, crystallized in our abstraction as "ideas," modify each other, so that by and large man's present is the result of his past. As memory transforms the past into the present, however, the past that is alive within us is also influenced by the elements that have since been added or are currently being formed. As a result, in our spiritual lives, the one-directional causality of time, which only presses forward, becomes an interactive process. Because the past is still preserved within us in its identical, recollected form, we arrive at the apparently paradoxical situation in which the present exerts an effect on the past just as the past does on the present. Our consciousness at any given moment usually consists of only a minimum of freshly generated material. For the most part it is nourished by recollected mental images; thus its overall picture consists of the interactive process or inter-active state of these recollections, which in a sense represent the whole of our life up to the present time, together with the mental images currently being generated. Thus within the conscious mind we have an interaction and an organic-personal oneness that far surpass our physical being in cohesion. And we cannot avoid conceptualizing the unconscious processes within us, on which the conscious processes are somehow based, as being in a constantly interactive state.

Mechanistic psychology is doubtless mistaken in describing mental images as *entities* that come and go, associating with and separating from one another, and so on. This kind of construct can be achieved only by abstracting the logically expressible elements from the continuous and integrated flux of our innermost life and endowing them with some sort of bodily existence, so that they appear as independent entities making up the very substance of this life themselves. The idea that a mental image is a clearly delineated, independently active or passive element is pure myth, mistakenly inspired by physical atomism. Nevertheless, for the time being I see no way of circumventing this dual conceptualization of the psyche. On the one hand, it is a single *process* surging forth in the unity of life, which has no dimension; on the other, it is a conglomerate of distinct *contents* that we must view as standing in complex relation to one another.

We should not lose sight of the symbolic, projectional character of the latter picture. Therefore, we should not regard a "mental image" as existing "as is" in the subconscious mind as if preserved in cold storage, rather like an actor waiting invisibly for his cue behind the scenes. And yet there is an inescapable and puzzling sense in which such a recollected image remains intact. Because this intactness applies to innumerable mental images and because none of them is absolutely and rigidly identical in content when it reappears in recollection, it must be assumed that processes of mutual influence and modification have occurred during this latent period. Thus the psychic elements within us that are somehow beyond our conscious mind are in a state of continuous interaction, and in this way forge themselves into the unity we call personality. The latter is not a merely stable center but a mutual penetration, a functional adaptation and transfer, an interrelationship of parts, a fusion within the sphere of all possible psychic contents. Thus, in contrast to the single psychic element, which as such seems dislocated and disconnected, our "personality" develops as a process that we describe by means of the form symbol of the interaction between all these elements.

Therefore we would be *perfect* personalities (in a formal sense) if this interaction were itself a perfectly unified whole, and if every psychic occurrence originated within this sphere. This is not the case, however. Our psyche is as much enmeshed in a world external to itself as is our physical body; influences are at work within it that cannot be accounted for by our psyche alone, and it would seem that some of its inner processes take up an external path and therefore do not have their full effect within the psyche itself. Just as our body does not conform to the concept of the organism in its purest form, neither does our soul fulfill the concept of personality. Thus, although this concept may well have derived psychologically from our experience of ourselves, it is nevertheless in essence "an idea," a category to which no single empirical being conforms entirely. The very fact that the form of our existence is one of temporal progression, requiring "memory" of the past in order to bring its content into an ever-fragmentary interaction—this fact alone prevents any unity of all its content, which would make us personalities in the absolute sense. The idea of the organism is realized fully in only one single concept: the totality of the universe itself, as this is defined as having nothing external to it that could break through the unified, interactive whole of all its elements. Similarly, the concept of God is the ultimate realization of personality: for God, as He is conceived of in the purely metaphysical terms of religion, knows no "memory" in the human, temporal sense, which always assumes its opposite, the act of forgetting. For Him there is no past, which carries its elements forward only as fragments into the interactive process of His present state; to one who does not need to "remember," there can be no such thing as time. The wholeness and unity of His being is not subject to the fragmentariness and incompleteness of temporal incoherence.

The "eternity" of God, as it is called, His being removed from temporal limitation, is the form that enables Him to be "personal" in the absolute sense. This does not impose on Him a human mould, but rather marks the very point that is beyond man's reach, the absolute cohesion and self-sufficiency of the total substance of His being. An entity that is part of a whole, such as man, can never be a perfect personality, because it interacts with external sources. This is the same principle in a juxtapositional form as the dependence of our existence on memory, the latter being in a sequential form: no single moment is a completely cohesive whole, each one depends on past and future, and therefore none is really a self-contained unit. It is quite mistaken to suppose that God is personality to the extent that man draws him down into his own confinement, for man's limiting factor is that he is part of a whole rather than the whole itself. His existence is not an integrated unity because it is divided temporally into incoherent moments associated only by memory; it is precisely this which prevents him from being a personality in the full sense of the term.

God fulfills the concept of personality for the very reason that the idea of God encompasses a genuine totality and a unique timelessness, an absolute cohesion of all the facets of His existence. In other words, God is personality by virtue of the fact that He surpasses man. Just as our own imperfect unity is borne mysteriously by the idea of a self, the true unity of universal being is crystallized in an ultimate self, the absolute personality. It would no doubt be true to assert, for example, that to attribute "personality" to God is the same as raising the concept of personality to divine status. We do not refer here, however, to the small-scale personality of man, but to the large-scale personality of the world—the ideal realization of all the determining characteristics of personality, which is inaccessible to man and thus accommodates religiousness. Because this religious sentiment holds true for the form of the universe, beyond the specific elements it binds together, its object is God—the ultimate sense of wholeness into which all these elements become merged.

Let us mention once more that whether God exists objectively or even whether He is believed in subjectively has nothing to do with this purely conceptual definition, for which the question of being or not being is irrelevant. This definition, however, places the choice between the pantheistic and the personalistic views of the divine principle on a new foundation. If one is to take the concept of personality seriously—interpreting it not as the limiting aspects of our own being but as that to which we have only limited access, as that which we, as inadequate beings, are *not*—this concept can be realized only as an absolute being: a being that is either one and the same as the totality of the world, *substantia sive Deus,* or a being that denotes this totality, comparable to the soul as ἐντελέχεια σώματος φυσικοῦ ὀργανικοῦ. Yet the pantheistic view brings out further problems and contradictions within the concept of God, for which its personal form can provide a solution.

In most of the history of religions, the significance of the divine principle is associated with the confrontation between the deity on the one hand and the religious person with his world on the other; the essential feature of the deity to whom we surrender is that He is *powerful*. Thus from the rawest of superstitions to the most sublime Christian speculation, this motif presupposes some independent existence to confirm that power—shaping, overcoming, guiding. A deity that is subsumed into a unity with the whole of existence cannot possibly possess any power, because there would be no separate object to which He could apply such power. This juxtaposition of God and the individual is equally necessary for the motif of love. If mystical passion seeks to penetrate its God to the point of unity, tearing down every barrier toward this goal, it might sense a deeper, more blissful love with every step toward such union. Yet it would be left in emptiness at the moment of total fulfillment, for in this absolute unity it would grasp only itself. If the idea of a duality were to disappear completely, all the possibilities of giving and taking, of loving and being loved, would vanish equally—possibilities on which religious bliss also depends, the soul being as it is.

Even where such bliss has been found and is now possessed, there is still in some spiritual dimension a sense of seeking and longing, or an echo of this sense. Even peace in God is gained only from a sense that He is still removed. But this sense that a juxtaposition is required for love, and especially for power, does not tally with the absoluteness of the divine being; for any independence of things, any nonbeing of God within them, is a limitation of His power, though the latter is supposed to be unlimited. Not one sparrow falls to the ground without God's will: surely this does not mean that He merely has no objections to what is happening like some passive observer of the world's course, but clearly that He is the instrumental, motive force behind everything that happens. Yet because everything is in incessant motion and because all apparent materiality is in constant oscillation, is there anything left in which God is *not* present? If the world is motion and if God is the moving force within every movement, then no part of the world is external to Him.

The work produced by the will of a *human* creator cannot, of course, form a part of that same will—the work of the will is distinct from the will itself; but this is only because man is confronted with a being, a material that he *encounters* and that he fashions. Yet if God really is all-powerful, and if *everything* happens by His will, then nothing is external to Him, and He is the being and becoming of all things. Thus it is quite arbitrary to claim that various aspects of reality are invested with His will to varying degrees; that certain phenomena display the "hand of God" while others supposedly elude Him, defiantly independent and "godforsaken." Is this not a projection onto reality of the disparities of our own knowledge, of the mixture of blindness and perception that characterizes our own view? If *one* aspect of reality is a reflection of God's will, then every other aspect must also be such a reflection. Neither the rigorously law-governed coherence of the cosmos nor the unity of God permits different parts of the world to have different relationships to Him. If even the sparrow falling to the ground is an expression of God's will, then it is the inevitable consequence that the world is totally embraced in His unity, and that there can be no mutual independence or distinctness of one from the other.

Such a dialectical process develops the systematic concept of God into a pantheistic concept. This process cannot end there, however, because indispensable religious values are based on the notion that God and the world or God and man are juxtaposed and distinct. This dialectical process, with all its repercussions, runs through the core of all religions that earnestly adhere to the absoluteness of a divine principle. But perhaps there is no need for a "reconciliation" of this contradiction between fusion and separation; perhaps this sense of being driven from one to the other is the only adequate expression of our relationship to the infinite, which we should not hope to be able to define with a neat formula. The only conception of God that provides a lucid symbol for this constellation is that of His *personality.* For it is surely the essence of personality that it consists of unlimited contents, of which every single item possesses a certain independence, and yet which are comprehended as the contents or products of an integrating unity. The self embraces all of its thoughts, feelings, and decisions as something emanating uniquely from itself, possible and real only within itself, pulse beats of its being; yet the self is *distinct from* each item of content and is not subsumed within it.

Yet the content is not subsumed within the self either, because the self *judges* every such object, accepts or rejects it, is master of it or not. This object is created by the self and is part of the self's life; this is precisely the remarkable relationship that is characterized by a sense of belonging, but that does not prevent detachment and independence. Even in the physical sphere the limb of a whole organism has a quite different relationship to its whole—closer yet freer—than does a part of a rigid, mechanical system; in the psychical sphere these contradictions take on a yet greater force. The more we feel ourselves each to be a fully developed *personality,* and the more one knows the self to be independent of each constituent part, the less likely one is to be thrown off balance by any particular content. Yet, at the same time, each component at this level is more independent in relation to the self in terms of its logical and ethical, its dynamic and historical legitimation; it is not drawn into the entire destiny of the self, which is determined by other factors. And yet the more we are a personality, the more we color the content of our lives with the distinct individuality of our own self, the more recognizable it is as belonging to us. In this regard the self is superior—not only in the sense of independence from specific things, but also in the sense of having control over them.

Any "personality" contains this duality and contradiction between the individual element and the unified whole, and this distinguishes it completely from phenomena that have an apparent outward similarity to it, such as the state. The state, however omnipotent it may be, can encompass only certain *parts* of the whole existence of its citizens. The form of existence realized by the soul as personality thus defeats all habitual categories of logic. The single element of the soul is rooted firmly in the self, and the self is alive within the core of this element. Yet each is quite distinct from the other, so that manifold forms of detachment and proximity, contrast and fusion are possible. This is not something that can be described; it can only be experienced. Only one analogy to this exists in the whole of mankind's history of ideas: the relationship between God and the world, a relationship that is difficult for logic to describe. Our empirical experience of personality is a pledge, so to speak, that there is no absurdity in that simultaneous experience of distinctness and unity which the religious consciousness senses continually. According to this duality, God must be *conceived* of as "personality" if He is to be conceived of at all: the oneness and the vitality of existence, which looks upon its individual products, exercising power over them, but which at certain times is not in control of their independence, dwelling within every single one and yet maintaining a detachment that has infinite stages between alienation or separation and innermost fusion. Personality signifies the center and the periphery, the unified whole and its parts, and this unique relationship between them: thus the personality of God is not a denial of pantheism but, as it were, simply pantheism itself come *alive*.

Just as the first-mentioned characteristic of personality—the integrated interaction of elements—was in no sense an anthropomorphism in its application to the divine principle, this second qualification is equally far from being an anthropomorphism. For although we experience this relationship of simultaneous union and detachment only within ourselves, it is nevertheless in essence a universal form of existence that is not bound to one particular manifestation but that can be realized in widely varying degrees of perfection. It is a category to which we assign the immediate fact of our existence, in order to express it and reflect on it. One can speak of an anthropomorphism of the divine only when a concept that is intrinsically associated with human experience and existence as such is applied to the transcendental. If, on the other hand, a concept is in itself on a higher plane than human existence—a conceptual absolute, as it were, providing us with the very means by which to interpret this existence with regard to the extent of its correspondence to this concept—this is the only kind of concept we can legitimately regard as being realized in its absolute form by the divine. Even if one basically rejects faith in the divine as faith in something that actually exists, it is nevertheless by no means an anthropomorphization to describe the idea of God in terms of personality. In fact, the opposite is true: in describing God in terms of personality we are classifying the human self in a subcategory of a quite general concept. This concept denotes a form of existence of which the human manifestation is merely a single, limited example, whereas God is the absolute fulfillment of this form on a universal scale.

Finally, it is possible to consider the essential nature of personality in another, as it were more concentrated form. It seems to me that the most crucial characteristic of the personal mind is its intrinsic splitting of itself into a subject and an object that are one and the same, its capacity to address itself in the first person as it addresses another in the second person. This is its self-consciousness, by which its own *function* becomes its *content,* and by which life fragments itself in order to rediscover itself, as it were—though fragmentation and rediscovery are simply ways of expressing as a temporal sequence something that in fact is a single act. This is the essential feature, or even the miracle, of the mind, that which makes it personal: it can reflect on itself as on a separate entity and still can remain in its unified state. The identity of knowing and known, such as is manifest in a person's knowledge of his own being and knowledge, is a fundamental phenomenon that goes far beyond the mechanical, numerical contrast of unity and duality. The course of life is such that each moment of a person's life is borne by some previous moment—two separate moments, yet *one* life in both, in which what has been created continues the process of creation, different and yet somehow still the same. In self-consciousness this temporally extended path is turned back on itself, finding its fundamental, timeless form. The profound difference between an organism and a mechanism is that in the former, multiplicity is merged into unity, or that in an organism a unity unfolds in a temporally and spatially differentiated life. This is precisely what characterizes the personal mind or consciousness and constitutes the very essence of its nature. For in that "interaction" which is the essence of all that is alive and all that is mental, self-consciousness—by which the subject becomes its own object—achieves its absolute form.

This also would appear to be the purest expression of the form symbolizing the unity of the divine being. Scholars of religious history claim that there has never been a completely pure monotheism. It seems as though the divine principle carries an inevitable tendency to divide — even if only in that God is often surrounded by seraphim or "spirits." His most perfect unity, as perceived in pantheism and to some extent in mysticism, is at the same time His most complete dispersal in the multiplicity of real phenomena. This formulation would appear to me to bring the concept of God closer to that of personality, though here one must be especially careful not to confuse the concept with anthropomorphism. Self-consciousness, by which thought divides itself within itself to become its own object while retaining its unity, is the fundamental feature of all thought, and its most concentrated, purest, and most assured form — the prototype, as it were, for every specific thought.

How can thought have an *object* and yet remain a self-contained process? How can it absorb a distinct entity while remaining entirely subjective? This obscure mystery of the mind is resolved if we consider that as self-consciousness it already harbors these dichotomies; the identity of subject and object is the form of the mind's own existence. Self-consciousness — although here only within the category of human thought — thus anticipates the very same division to which the divine principle is subjected, while retaining its metaphysical unity — and all the more so, the more advanced the stage of religious development. The motif of the "self-consciousness of God" thus runs through the whole of the philosophy of religion; very often it is simply another expression or interpretation of the "personality of God." The divine principle cannot be conceived of as absolute unity, for unity fails to provide inspiration for our imagination. It can be considered to fall within the same categorial problem as the self-conscious personality: how to split itself within itself and gain a separate opposite that is motion, effectiveness, and life, and yet retain its unity. This idea might be shaped by the speculative imagination as a kind of immanent pantheon, such as the Christian trinity, or as pantheism, which regards the wealth of processes within the world as nothing but the extension of divine unity to its own object, as suggested by Spinoza's mysticism: our love of God would be a part of God's love of Himself. But this concept of personality requires a high degree of abstraction if we are not to become caught up in an anthropomorphization of God. This latter aspect of personality [anthropomorphization] in particular appears to be identified totally with the *spirit,* but the divine principle cannot be reduced to this concept. To describe God as spirit is merely an inverse materialism, defining the absolute as a particular substance.

If the concept of personality is to apply to God, however, it must be framed in such a general form that the self-conscious mind—the only instance of this form to which we have empirical access—can be regarded only as a special case of that general concept. Of course the only way *we* have of perceiving a subject to be its own object is in the self-conscious mind, but the higher form must be distinguished from this particular substratum if the concept is to be applied to an absolute being that subsumes the totality of existence. It is not possible to visualize an image that might give us any clearer notion of our conceptual requirements in this respect. But if there is a particular way in which we must imagine the divine being, it is in the form of personality, though by no means that of human personality. It is a distinct entity beyond monolithic unity, interactive with something separate from itself, yet preserving unbroken unity and remaining itself in the "self-imbued" relational totality of the world as an identical subject and object. This is not an anthropomorphism: it does not take man's confinement to a merely *psychic* form of unified duality and apply it to God. Indeed the reverse is true: "personality" has an entirely formal or abstract definition, which can be realized in the form of an absolute being only in this abstraction, whereas a less perfect one-dimensional mental form is a part of *our* lives. Therefore, it would be accurate to state that God is not man on a large scale, but man is God on a small scale.

Thus once again we have defined the principle that has

guided this essay. To be able to impose order and values on the realities of our life, we draw on *ideas;* our consciousness of these ideas results psychogenetically from the coincidental and fragmentary state of empirical life. These ideas, however, essentially possess an ideational independence and a cohesive wholeness from which the contents of our human existence—as if by an act of subtraction—draw their denotation, their measure, their particular form. Whether this actually happens, and to what extent, is a question answered by empirical life itself; it does not affect the description of the ideational categories, their conceptual interrelationship, and their logical and normative significance. Insofar as a divine being is to be conceived of in terms of what it actually represents as a concept, our only point of reference must be these ideas, though in their most absolute and purest form. It cannot be a question of *degree:* we cannot speak of God as possessing more power, more justice, more perfection than man. This kind of quantitative comparison obviously takes man as its starting point and therefore is anthropomorphistic. To the person of faith, God is the idea of power, justice, and perfection in the form of being; His content is that which stands above the relative existence of man as man's ideational form; He is the pure meaning from which our relative, imperfect, and impure lives gain their meaning and their form.

I feel quite sure that this attitude of the person of faith exists within every religiously mature person as a feeling that can be expressed only in logical paradoxes: what is essential is not that God is above man, but that man is below God. The former statement is taken for granted, so to speak, but life's sense of religion and of the religious task of man is derived from the latter. In the relationship between God and man, only the second element is relative. The first is absolute: the reality of that conceptual ideal by which man estimates the form, degree, and meaning of his relativity. Whether or not this reality is believed is a matter for religion, but not for the philosophy of religion. The latter can speak—again a logical paradox—only of that which is often enough of secondary importance to the religious person: for the philosophy of religion can treat only of the conceptual content of the divine principle, not of whether it exists in reality. It has been my task to illuminate the concept of personality, precisely because it seems to be based so firmly on an upward-oriented, human perspective, and to outline what, for human thought, are the only possible determining characteristics of a divine being. The concept of personality need only be expressed to its pure essence to show that it belongs to that conceptual order which is not characterized by a human perspective but which rather confers meaning and form on everything below it; it stands in much the same relation to the specific objects of human activity as God's existence stands to man's from a religious point of view.

God's existence, however, is so independent of man's and is nourished from such different spiritual and material sources that the philosophy of religion—although certainly able to claim to define God in terms of "personality"—has not the slightest authority to claim that God exists. If philosophy stays within this domain, it remains distinct from unwarranted speculation as to the *existence* of God. Such speculation is not content to confine itself to its proper realm, namely the conceptual order relating to the *content* of a state of being, whereas this state of being as such can flow only from quite different sources. As long as the philosophy of religion does not enter into improper competition with religion itself, it retains the legitimacy of a painting that portrays the inner logic and the meaning of details and interrelationships of the concrete world, and, like a work of art, remains distinct from any accidental reality. Speculation, on the other hand, might be compared to a perspective that employs the means adequate for constructing a conceptual order but insufficient for constructing either the reality of facts or the reality of faith, yet that nonetheless attempts to usurp the creative powers of the latter.

**PART 3** *Religion and Art*

The historical threads with which religion and art are inter-woven have been pursued countless times. How the require-ments of ritual caused deific images to be created, how poetic forms developed from religious ceremony and the invocation of the gods, how growth and decline in the development of reli-gion had a parallel and often completely inverse influence on art—all this has become part of the recognized stock of cultural history. Still in need of elucidation, however, are the motivating forces rooted in the very essence of religion and art, by which the two attract or repel each other, and which make all these historical links appear to be more or less perfect realizations of more profound, more fundamental associations.

We are often forced to impose the spatial metaphor of prox-imity and distance on spiritual relationships, even though this symbol, physically measurable as it is, remains ultimately alien to the essential nature of such relationships. One hopes that this metaphor at least is sufficiently comprehensible, however, to allow one to describe the similarities of religious and artistic behavior thus: both transport their object to a distance far be-yond any immediate reality in order to bring this object very close to us, closer than immediate reality ever could bring it.

The purer the form religion takes, free of other areas of spiritual life that blend it with shortcomings and limitations, the more it thrusts its God out into the "beyond." His distance from all that is tangible in the reality of our world is the most extreme form of that "distance" to which *man* in his superiority consigns all those who are not comparable to himself. But this God both remains and does not remain at such a distance: it is as if the soul were to take a step backwards, in an approach run, in order to be able to embrace Him all the more closely as its most intimate possession, ultimately to be joined in mystical unity with Him.

Art similarly reflects this dual relationship to our reality. It possesses that quality of distinctness from life itself, a release through contrast, in which the representation of things in their pure form makes any point of contact with our reality impossible, whether or not they are appreciated subjectively. But the very fact that the contents of our existence and of our imagination are removed from us in this way means that they are brought closer to us than in their empirical form. Whereas everything in the real world can be included in our lives as the tools and materials of life, the work of art remains completely detached. Ultimately and at a deeper level, however, all these empirical realities remain alien to us; even the relationship between our soul and that of another person, our longing to give and take, is hindered by a hopeless isolation. The work of art is alone in having the capacity to become ours completely, and only in this form can we have complete access to another soul: by being more its own than anything else, it is more ours than anything else could be.

It is customary for us to feel that the contents of our lives are not "ours" as such but require some existential significance, some "fate," in order to bring them closer to us. Only the God we believe in and the art we take delight in are given for our complete spiritual possession from the beginning and by their mere being. And even though two people who are deeply in love are conscious of being predestined for each other by the fate that brings them together, such love is nevertheless distinct from predestination and fate by virtue of its complete individuality: the soul binds itself only to this particular person precisely because of his or her uniqueness. But when the person of faith knows himself to be at one with his God through his mere existence, or when the person moved by a work of art senses it to be like his own inner necessity, it is no longer individual peculiarities taking effect, but those basic layers in which the self comes into full being, yet nevertheless feels itself to be the bearer of more fundamental principles and of a sense of no longer being bound to the particular and the individual. This seems to me to be the ultimate similarity of form through which religion always anticipates art and art always stimulates religious sentiment: only these two can bring about a state of being that exists solely for its own sake and can become the innermost possession of a soul, as if utterly natural and foreordained.

This essential similarity between the form of religious life and that of art manifests itself in diverse ways in various cultures. It is rather as if the intensification of this similarity in Christianity sometimes makes it appear to be a complete contrast. Of all the major religions, Christianity certainly has the strongest sense of tension between the proximity and the distance of God. At the same time, however, it has the greatest reconciliation between the two, because in Christianity there is a relationship of the *heart* to God that displays its triumphant strength in the very boundlessness of the metaphysical distance it spans. This would seem to fulfill the need of some souls to create an enormous distance between themselves and some aspect of their lives and then to draw it into themselves totally; in fact, Christianity appears to satisfy this need so completely that the corresponding spiritual fulfillment offered by art seems to be superfluous, or even to represent some inadmissible rivalry. That Christianity has so often rejected art directly cannot be attributed to the ascetic repudiation of sensory stimulation only, nor merely to a lack of aesthetic culture. In fact it can be ascribed, among other motives, to this instinct: the soul no longer needs art, for it already has the means by which to stretch out into the realm beyond empirical existence and to draw it all back into itself.

At the same time, the characters and events of the Christian tradition, as well as the physical expression that its particular spiritual states evoke, offer thematic motifs that almost appear to be designed specifically for the arts. Humility, prayer, fervent rapture—all of these are particularly effective in drawing the body together, keeping the extremities close to the trunk, and thus enhancing the wholeness and symbolic unity of the body. Even the reaching out of arms in prayer is quite distinct from the arms' merely being stretched out; the latter interferes with the cohesion of the image. For in prayer either the hands are joined, which lends the image a very marked sense of cohesion, or, when they are spread apart, they reach out toward some ideal point of focus at which the lines of their inner movements converge — just as it is said of parallel lines that they meet in "infinity."

In all good art the whole frame of the human body is tightly held together, and this is one of the requirements thanks to which the appeal of a mere pictorial image becomes a symbol for spiritual norms. For we ask of the individual that all his outward expressions be guided and characterized by some center, not fragmented anarchically, without reference to the unity of his person. In the same way, we require of any plastic representation of a human being that the limbs give the impression of being absolutely obedient to every impulse of central unity, not untouched by any of the currents of emotion and animation that imbue the whole person. When the entire body is infused with the movements of the soul, making it a true embodiment of personality, this phenomenon is raised to the level of sensory perception by means of the unity and centricity of the frame, the sense that the actions of each limb are determined by the emotional center. When we say of a human form that it is "animated," this is simply another way of expressing the artistic requirement for its cohesion and sense of unity.

The absolute domination of the soul, for which Christianity lives, is thus expressed adequately in all those physical attitudes which anticipate their artistic form even empirically because they fulfill these conditions of unity and cohesion by their very nature. The particular significance of the visual form as an expression of a spiritual condition lies in strict formal concentration which is pervaded by powerful inner emotion. This contrasts with the Buddha figures of Indian and Japanese sculpture, in which the artistic unity of appearance is utterly perfect, even though the spirituality expressed is not actually one of inner movement. Rather we are dealing with absolute resignation, with the withdrawal of the soul into complete immobility. This, of course, is pure unity, because there can be no more expansion of life here. The gestures characteristic of Christianity, by contrast, convey a powerful sense of passion, even though this passion is oriented toward a single, most inward and vital point.

A particularly pronounced and effective illustration is to be found in a phenomenon of Christian mythology that the artistic instinct identified from the very beginning as having unique formal significance in artistic terms: the Virgin Mary with her child. The inner harmonization and integration of all the elements of being, the concentrated unity of life of which I spoke earlier—this finds its most direct expression in feminine nature. Womankind generally is thought to possess a more undifferentiated nature—whether this assumption is everywhere and always correct is not at issue here. A woman's instincts and energies are felt to be more uniform and less fragmented than those of a man, and more centered on a single focal point that fires all else. In keeping with this idea, a woman's natural physical appearance—even more so her appearance in art—is expected to possess complete centripetal unity and harmony; her gestures are required to be well integrated, not reaching out beyond herself. Even if such gestures have an immediate focal point outside herself, they nevertheless ultimately point inward, joining the full circle of harmony with everything else that she has.

This harmony is apparently dissolved by the Madonna's association with the child; she now sees the meaning of her existence in a being outside herself. And yet we have here the mystery of motherliness itself: this unity remains unperturbed, and the child is both the mother's nonself and her self at one and the same time. Here the conflict between existing for oneself and existing for another person is resolved, but not in the egoistical sense whereby the self is extended to include another person, as it were, and yet remains egoistical. Here a more elevated meaning of life is revealed: only by being oriented toward a deeper sense of purpose, which has taken on its *own existence,* is the individual's inner coherence given its full power and consecration. When the mother focuses on the child, her unity apparently is disturbed; yet it is in fact only this that completely preserves such unity.

This spiritual structure of motherliness is the central formal problem to be addressed in a pictorial representation of the Virgin Mary with the Infant. Where this has been solved successfully, the woman's appearance is an image of absolute unity *in itself,* even though *in combination with the child* it offers an artistically rounded and completed form. This is the aesthetic and visual realization of one being joined together with another as a whole, not merely as a limb or a fragment, but finding its own supreme harmony in this way. The distinctive significance of the infant Jesus precludes any mere animalistic pairing of mother and child, in which the child is still a *pars viscerum;* that very distinctiveness brings to a climax the tension between the two and the problem of creating a visual image of the religious-metaphysical relationship between the Madonna and her child. With its solution to this problem, art opened up a whole new realm of forms—forms that allowed the depiction of the individual to gain its highest significance when it was set in relation to another individual.

Here we have the general configuration of Christian mythology, in which it differs from ancient myths: each individual relates to others in a specific and distinctive way, which largely determines that individual's own significance. St. John is there for Jesus' sake, just as Mary and the angels are, at different levels; Jesus is there for the sake of everyone; the saints for the believers or unbelievers; and the Church embraces all the various planes of Christian life in an organism of interacting parts. Thus the whole sphere of holy figures is pervaded by a network of mutual relationships deriving from their most profound religious nature and shaping it at the same time, whereas the interrelationships between the classical gods and heroes are either purely externally consanguineous or are anecdotal, with little consequence for their religious significance. This is why painting is just as characteristic of Christian religious art as sculpture is of ancient art: the former offers forms of depiction for the relationships between several personalities, whereas the latter lends itself to the representation of single, self-contained figures.

The problem of the Child appears to be no less revolutionary than the problem of the Madonna within the development of artistic forms. The body of a child—quantitatively insignificant, undifferentiated, and with little capacity for powerful or vivid expression—is nonetheless to become *visually* the legitimate center of the picture, the dominant and meaning-giving force within it. It is fascinating to trace the means by which painters have overcome this contradiction. In the remarkable tondo in Berlin, for example, Botticelli gives the child an especially strong emphasis by placing it in a horizontal position, when all the other figures in the picture are upright. Andrea del Sarto achieves the same effect in his great Madonna in the Uffizi by depicting the Child as the only lively, mobile element among figures who are all standing immobile. Sometimes the child's nakedness makes it stand out particularly powerfully and sensually among the other, dressed figures. In the apse painting, Michelangelo uses psychological as opposed to formal means: he conveys the vivid impression that this child is what is most important to its parents, and this makes it quite naturally the most important element in the whole picture. Here, as is frequently the case, the fact that the physical gestures and stances of the other characters are directed toward the Child immediately causes one to conclude that this small being obviously must possess the superiority to justify being placed at the center and revered from all sides.

This particular problem of artistic portrayal corresponds to a similar difficulty which arises at the end of Jesus's life. When on the cross, or when being taken down from the cross, Jesus appears not to have the strength to act as the inspiring force for all the vitality around him. Visually, the corpse is like some material object, subject to mere gravity, and would seem to lack the upward orientation of the spirit required to conquer physical heaviness. As a result, the superiority assigned to this figure is not made immediately perceptible in sensory terms. The artistic means of dealing with this discrepancy in a painting are similar to those mentioned in relation to the previous problem. Once again, the nakedness of the figure especially has an accentuating effect; also precisely this body is the only motionless one among many others moved by passion. Finally, the mere representation of the effect again is all the more striking and powerful because it stands in contrast to its apparent visual justification.

Because of certain imponderables, the image of Christ therefore achieves what it actually should not be able to achieve. This is the artistic expression of the profound paradox of Christianity: demands are made of the soul that should in fact be impossible to fulfill. The mortal being is to adopt transcendental values, and perfection is expected of the imperfect. The task is made so difficult that it seems insoluble; that a solution is found after all, or at least is conceived of and depicted visually in the representation of "holiness," allows the immeasurable power of the soul to unfold. It is as if the stage of being "possible" is simply omitted: confronted with the absolute demands of Christianity, the soul finds itself in a state of impossibility, and yet at the same time in a state of fulfillment and perfection. Christ as "mediator" seems to make superfluous the stage of "being able"; an ideal link comes into effect, which conveys that the soul is achieving something of which it is actually incapable. This fundamental characteristic of Christianity, of which the intellectual form is *credo quia absurdum,* has been taken up by art in the sense that powerful effects are conveyed by images that would not appear to be capable of exerting such effects.

Less absolute, but of no less artistic interest, is the way in which Christianity has succeeded in its art in avoiding the apparently inevitable choice in depicting figures of sacred history: between historical verisimilitude and the imaginative creativity of the individual artist. There have always been considerable difficulties in the artistic portrayal of outstanding historical personalities, who inevitably can be visualized only with a certain vagueness, both because of the wealth and diversity of associations and because of their distance from us in time. If we are told that a male figure in a work of art is Phidias or Plato or Charlemagne, the effect is often disappointing to the point of awkwardness or even humor. Our mental image of such personalities is subject to considerable variation and centers on a certain fixed core of associations, though these are of uncertain contour. Any concrete pictorial representation confines this mental image, to an unacceptable degree. Indeed, because of the firm limitations of anything visual, such a representation *cannot* satisfy the demands of our imagination and is both an impoverishment and an assault by comparison. When a genuinely historical portrait is handed down, this difficulty no longer applies, because reality is more persuasive than these vague hoverings of the imagination, or else it enables us to focus the imagination onto the unrefuted pictorial representation.

The art of the Christian Church has avoided this dualism impressively by creating consistent types for its figures, which, by virtue of their specific concentration of features, assume the function of historical truth. We may not believe that the unprepossessing man in the chiton is Phidias, or that the figure holding the imperial regalia is Charlemagne. Yet the tradition of Christian art has nonetheless achieved its own equivalent: we believe —with the kind of "belief" that might apply in the conceptual sphere of art—that the man in the blue garment is Christ, that the figure bound to the tree is Saint Sebastian, and that the lady with the drooping lyre is Saint Cecilia. But the sense of actuality that church tradition has breathed into these phenomena in retrospect, so to speak, is now broad enough and universal enough to allow for every possible individual elaboration, artistic nuance, or stylistic variation. This is the enormously significant creation of the *type of an individual.* If the artist's distinctive way of visualizing historical personalities generally seems constrained, pitiful, and unconvincing, this particular combination overcomes the problem: religious tradition has created belief in these types and thus has replaced actual historical truth, usually the only way of overcoming this failing. Yet because as we are dealing here not with knowledge but with belief, there remains unbounded freedom for individual artistic creativity.

Thus in all of these ways the spiritual substance of Christianity has caused art to seek out new forms. Formal problems of composition and profile, how to convey the plasticity of a human figure and distribute points of emphasis within a painting—all these problems became particularly critical in this context, and their solution has borne fruit for all kinds of artistic subjects beyond the religious sphere. Finally, however, I should like to refer to one further example from among the new *themes* that art has gained from Christianity, and in which the capacity for its expression was not achieved through purely formal means. I mean the depiction of *suffering:* only since Christianity can anguish in art be justified through ultimate profundity in its artistic, visual portrayal. Of course, ancient art offers such examples as Niobe and Laocoön. Yet in ancient art, suffering is an external fate, precisely the opposite of that deep-rooted necessity by which it is characterized in Christianity: the fruit of the soul itself, or the tone it must sound when, summoned to an eternal fate, it is bound by mortality. On the other hand, ancient art can offer the Amazon and Antinous. Yet the painful emotion here is *sorrow,* and sorrow is a reaction to suffering, not the primary pain of fate itself but its reflex throughout what one might call the more general planes of the soul. Thus sorrow possesses an inner detachment even as an empirical event; its separation from direct involvement in fate itself makes it seem ideally suited to artistic rendering. The achievement of Christian art, however, is to have found ways of giving aesthetic potential and artistic form to immediate suffering that has not yet been transformed into sorrow.

Christianity has made positive many values that in other spheres of life, and often in other religions, are purely negative. The renunciation of earthly goods and everything physical is not merely an act of liberation; it does not only remove obstacles that hinder the soul in aspiring to its eternal fate. This renunciation is of itself something valuable, a precious possession of the soul. At the very least it is a part of the soul's path, not merely the casting off of a burden along this path. Furthermore, moral devotion and self-denial are not just the realization of an objective moral code that stands in opposition to selfishness. They are a direct elevation of the soul; self-denial is in itself a form of self-gain. Death is not merely liberation from the burden of life; Christ's sacrifice shows, rather, how death is the climax of life itself, its actual consecration and the stage of development for which the soul is destined between this life and the hereafter, positively extended, so to speak. Likewise, suffering is in no sense at all a negative state to Christianity, a debit on life's balance sheet. This is an interpretation that other philosophies of life use either to dismiss Christianity out of hand or to claim that it attaches a minus sign to the whole of human existence. On the contrary, suffering is an integral element of religious life. For it is precisely in its initial realization in our world and in its clash with the laws and powers of mortal life that God's kingdom is bound to produce suffering: this is why the *just* must suffer and why those who labor and are heavy laden shall find salvation. Thus, unlike in the tradition of ancient Greece, from a Christian point of view suffering is something for which one does not grieve, however little anguish is allowed to diminish its terrible solemnity.

This positive significance has deprived suffering of the character of *depression* that excludes it from art. If suffering is no more than one of life's troughs, it stands in contradiction to the exaltation of life that art represents. This does not apply to poetry, which can give suffering reconciliation and the potential to reach any height and stature through its capacity to create a continuum of moods and fortunes. But the visual arts, depending on a single moment of perception, can overcome their contradiction to suffering only when suffering itself has been elevated to be a positive motivation in life. In the Passion of Christ and the anguish of the martyrs, pain is no longer the hostile destroyer of life but a heightening toward a unique intensity. Suffering is thus imbued with a purpose that gives it a new worth and mission, canceling out its depression and ugliness. In this way, Christianity has discovered the aesthetic value of suffering and has bestowed upon its religious significance the language of visual depiction.

The claim that religion has "stimulated" art in this way or has given it a new mission can be acceptable only if it is based on a more profound consideration. In themselves, religion and art are in fact unconnected. Indeed, in their ideal forms, so to speak, they cannot meet or overlap with each other, because each expresses the whole of existence in its own particular language. One can view the world from a religious perspective or from an artistic one; one can see it practically or scientifically. The subject matter remains the same, always seen as a uniform yet unique cosmos but from a different point of view. Our soul, however, with its short-lived impulses and fragmentary abilities, is unable to fashion any of these worlds into the integrated whole it requires; each of these souls remains dependent on random stimuli that one or another of its fragments plants within us. These worldviews may be lacking a self-sufficient completeness in their content, and yet this lack is precisely what creates the most profound vitality and spiritual relationships, for it directs each to the other for drawing on the impulses, contents, and tasks that each could find within itself, were its inner structure perfectly complete. While art accepts having such a service provided for it by religion, as these few examples show, art of course reveals that whichever reality it may produce might be lacking in absolute artistic creativity. Yet in this way art empowers the soul to supplement one world with the other and thereby to experience itself as the point of union, to be the force that has the potential for nourishing one of these currents from the other, because each of them in itself flows from the soul.

In the history of mankind, the essence of religion manifests itself in two basic forms. For that which constitutes religion—God and doctrine, ritual and Church—causes the religious individual, confronted with all this and reacting to it in a receptive or creative way, either seeking his own salvation or dedicating himself to it unselfishly, to initiate a twofold current within the essence of religion that can lead to complete fission. On the one hand, the *objectivity* of the facts of religion and of the Church, a self-contained world constructed according to its own laws, entirely indifferent to the individual who may only accept it and look up to it. On the other hand, religion as something that is located entirely within the subject's *inner life*. Whether or not these transcendental truths and cults exist metaphysically, their religious significance is to be found entirely within the qualities and the stirrings of the individual soul. These spiritual qualities may be inspired by the truths and cults, but they also may well give truths and rituals their meaning, breathing life into them. In the former case the quality of religiousness is a clear juxtaposition of deity and soul, which only subsequently, as it were, becomes a mutual acceptance. In the latter, religiousness is itself a form of spiritual life issuing from the most profound individual creativity and self-responsibility, though it possesses a metaphysical significance and grandeur whose religious quality takes it beyond the individual subject.

The greatest historical realization of this objectivity of the religious world is Catholicism; it is not possible to identify an equivalent for the other source of religious existence. This is quite understandable, because the dogma, ritual, and institutions that make religion historically visible can have at most only secondary importance for anyone to whom religion is an experience, a conduct or coloring of life itself, or a direct spiritual relationship with God. This relationship, by nature, can unfold only within the soul. Clearly, this kind of religiosity does not manifest itself outside the individual and therefore cannot become a general historical phenomenon. Neither is it represented by Protestantism; where, too, certain entirely objective facts of faith exist that are not located within the religious soul yet have this soul as their object: the universal rule of a personal God, the salvation won by Christ for mankind, the destinies that are assigned to the soul by the factual-religious structure of existence. If subjective religiosity were to be realized in an absolutely pure form (as it might never be, just as there can be no purely objective religion: each of these forms always occurs in some kind of combination with the other), it would be in the process of life itself, in the way the religious person lives each hour of his life, not in some specific content or in the belief in certain external realities.

One cannot claim by any means that these two opposed currents of religious life have divided Christian art neatly between themselves; however, the degree to which each occurs in a pure form or blended with the other might be represented as a scale on which each religious work of art could be located. *Byzantine* art depicts the transcendental world entirely objectively. In the mosaics of Ravenna, the characters and symbols of the Christian mysteries are portrayed in their metacosmic glory, completely indifferent to the human subjects experiencing them. There, man as a religious being—including the artist himself—has become completely devoid of subjectivity. Before him there stands an imposing array of self-sufficient divine forces that do not depend on individual feelings or spiritual destiny whether as a point of departure or of culmination for their visualization.

The *Trecento* has a different position on that scale. In the portraits of saints by Duccio, Orcagna, and some of their lesser contemporaries, the flawless grandeur is imbued with a tone of human lyricism. The transcendental sphere is not simply an unquestioned, objective power bearing down on man; man also responds to it with his own emotion. Thus the expression of religious *life*—however fragile and restrained—finds its way into the portrayal of transcendental facts. The relationship between objective and subjective religiosity shifts also in the art of the *High Renaissance,* because there the greater vitality and naturalism of depiction do not give it any enhanced expression of a personal, spiritual dynamic. Michelangelo is a completely isolated and atypical artist in this respect, and I do not include him in these remarks. But Leonardo and Raphael, Fra Bartolommeo and Andrea del Sarto all display remarkable objectivity in their depiction of saints. I feel that they are indeed closer to this pole of objectivity than was the Trecento, however much the rigor and the sacred dignity of the Trecento distinguish it from the Cinquecento. One really does not gain the impression that some religious spirituality has spontaneously influenced these compositions. Even where it is not purely aesthetic considerations that have prevented all other spiritual forces from making themselves felt, the religious purpose of such works still derives solely from the portrayal of a divine or historical existence—determined by its own center, its own immanence, not by the devotion or passion or dedication of an individual soul.

The peculiar ability of the human mind to step outside itself, as it were, and to view or to think from a different perspective is very powerful in the religious domain as well; in Renaissance art this ability was brought to bear unreservedly. I also include Rubens here; his Ildefonso altar piece might be said to reach the very peak of religious objectivity, precisely because of its perfect worldliness. The Divine Mistress displays the same noble, representative existence as does the prince who worships her; between the two, in fact, there is only a difference of degree within the same dimension, scaled down and concentrated, as it were. To have represented the divine in such a work as being determined by a personal religiosity would have been as inappropriate as it would have been incongruous with the views of the time for the Kaiser to have been elected directly by his subjects. Transcendental splendor is indeed given a human form here, but because the artist does this by means of the sociological label of "nobility," his refusal to allow any personal, subjective religiosity to permeate his art almost takes a deliberate, willful form.

*Rembrandt* is located at the very opposite end of the scale. All his religious paintings, etchings, and drawings have but a single theme: *the religious individual.* He does not visibly portray the artifacts of faith; wherever Jesus is depicted, it is never with the character of transcendental reality, but with that of empirical, human reality: his love, his teaching, his despair in Gethsemane, and his suffering. The objective existence of the divine as something that the man of faith can accept only by basking in its splendor—this has disappeared in Rembrandt's art. The religiousness he portrays is the *piety* generated by the individual soul in a variety of forms. This soul may be stimulated by transcendental powers, embraced by divine being and determined by it—but it is not this that Rembrandt depicts. What he shows us goes a stage beyond the transcendental: it is the condition created by the soul on the basis of its own individual strengths, a condition that can exist only within human souls and can be expressed only by mortal, human bodies. Though all the transcendental substance of faith may be real and (objectively speaking) the individual human being and his condition may be as insignificant as a grain of sand compared to such an absolute power, *religion* can come about only as the result of a relationship between the human soul and these supernatural phenomena. Religion always consists in the individual soul's contribution to such a relationship, the soul's own share in the existence of it. In theoretical terms, this is the fundamental principle of Rembrandt's religious art. For the first time in the history of art, this source of religious inspiration achieves pure predominance: whatever the object of faith, its metaphysical basis, or the substance of its dogma, religion here is a striving or a condition of the human soul.

The only other artist one might mention alongside Rembrandt in this respect is *Fra Angelico,* because in his work the artistic focus is also on the religious person as such. Ultimately, however, the religious content of his work, as well, is a universal element that hovers above the individuals portrayed and bears down on them; their experience of it is essentially passive. Here again, *dogma* is interwoven too closely with the purely spiritual process of piety to allow a sense of timeless religiousness to be captured, as it is in Rembrandt's work. It is true of the Middle Ages in general that piety resembles a substance that is poured out, permeating individual human beings. With Rembrandt, however, it is always generated afresh from the very depths of each individual soul. People are no longer in an objectively religious world; they are subjectively religious in an objectively indifferent world. Time and time again Rembrandt portrays biblical scenes that one is almost disinclined to regard as religious art, so devoid are they of any dogmatic, transcendental element: the experiences of Tobias, of the good Samaritan, and of the prodigal son, even Jesus' youth interpreted in the style of the petty bourgeoisie. Religiousness is a quality of these figures—an inner attribute, just like their wisdom or stupidity, their energy or their indolence. They may believe or act as they wish: piety is a determining factor of their subjective being as such, a quality that shines out all the more clearly as a distinctive coloring of their own personality because it manifests itself in the earthliness of their behavior. This religiosity is not bound to any specific content; it is not concerned with a mortal life and an afterlife. It depends not on a *terminus ad quem* but only on its *terminus a quo.* Wherever else religious values have been expressed in human form, either man has been deified or God has been anthropomorphized. Rembrandt goes beyond these alternatives because the element of religion in his art is not the objective relationship between man and God but that distinctive inner state of being within man which makes this relationship possible and from which it derives. For this reason, Rembrandt's figures are as far as possible removed from any religiosity of a "law," insofar as this law is universal and has become embodied in the Church dominating the individual.

This characteristic of his work suggests that Rembrandt became the focus of a general trend that was gathering momentum at that time. Among the Dutch *"Collegiates"* of the seventeenth century there was a deep mistrust of what the existing churches represented; it even went so far as complete rejection of all confessionalism. There emerged a religious subjectivism that allowed the individual the greatest possible scope for differentiation; thus even Calvinism, though rigidly objective and regulated, reached the point of regarding itself as a kind of individually fashioned religion, an intimate possession closely bound up with the individual's personal existence.

This absence of an objective, universal character of religion provides the deeper reason for which Rembrandt's conception of religious personalities is so far removed from any statuary portrayal. Sculpture is the nonindividual art form: it is the art of the most universal forms, at least until Rodin. This explains why in the Romanesque Renaissance even the painted figures often resemble statues; indeed, in certain cases this is even a typical feature. The universality of content provided by Catholicism found its equivalent in the universality of form provided by art, but Rembrandt's sensibility was not in tune with the problem of universality and therefore did not accommodate the artistic forms that culminated in sculpture. The religiosity of Rembrandt's figures does not lack this character of universality only because of the abstractness of universality or because religious *life* (in contrast to religious *content*) can be a quality only of the individual; it lacks it also because such universality is a domination and a violation of the individual. Not only is the law universal: what is universal is also law. In the Ravenna paintings of divine and holy beings — insofar as a relationship to the mortal sphere can be read into them in any way — it is precisely the aura of *authority* exuded by religion and by the Church that cannot fail to be noticed. Such works proclaim what is true and absolute, universality as the one and only law. Rembrandt's figures are so far removed from this universal unity because their religiousness is not the aura of the doctrinal content of faith (though such content is by no means denied) but a process of life itself, a function that can be fulfilled only within the individual.

This quality manifests itself in quite an extraordinary way in several of Rembrandt's depictions of Jesus. In a number of etchings, Jesus is portrayed as a boy who is insignificant and almost overpowered by those around him; in the Berlin picture of the Samaritan woman He is hardly more than a mere shadow, lacking substance in contrast to the forceful woman, who appears to be rooted firmly in the earth. And yet if one dwells on it only a moment longer, one realizes that this weak, wavering figure in fact is the only one possessing true strength. All of the strong, substantial figures are unstable and appear to be uprooted by comparison, as if only He, not they, stood firmly on the ground that is in fact mankind's. And it is not some transcendental radiance which makes this possible, not some sign indicating that the Redeemer belongs to a different order in the objective, metaphysical sense. It is simply that Jesus possesses the stronger—indeed the strongest—*religiosity,* that unconditional inner certainty which is a quality of his humanity. This quality is present in mankind as the result, or as one aspect, of Jesus' religiosity. In such instances, Jesus is simply the most highly developed of Rembrandt's religious figures, who can be differentiated from the nonreligious figures only by their personal spirituality. Such spirituality might derive divine graces from some power of metaphysical provenance, but this external power is not what the artist portrays. Instead he limits his problem to the spiritual state of the individual, whereby the transcendental origins of this state may be integrated into it so completely that they are no longer specifically recognizable as such.

Precisely this *certainty of the foundation of life* expressed in Rembrandt's portrayal of religiosity renders its subjectivism more than mere randomness or some transient "mood" that the subject might entertain by himself without its having any objective significance. What seems to me to be truly great and unique here is that the religious conduct that remains solely within the individual human being is conveyed as an eternal quality. To be able to comprehend this conception of religion, one cannot in any way determine the objectivity of its values by placing them outside the individual. The religious quality of the subject is of course an objective phenomenon itself; it is a state of being that has a metaphysical significance in its own right. The negative, degrading sense of the "subject" arises only when its whole status is allowed to be determined by an *opposite*, where the habits of empirical thought tend to separate, to find opposites, and to divide into large and small. Other depictions of the passion and ecstasy that overcome human beings confronted with a divine revelation, manifestation, or message may be subjective, in the sense of transitory and random, from the subject's own perspective. But wherever religious reality is rooted in the subject's very being, or rather where it is the subject's being, the person's religiosity is itself objective; this quality, once fixed, makes the existence of the world as such of much greater value, irrespective of temporal limitations. The religiousness portrayed in Rembrandt's art is thus interpreted as follows: it is not an element or a particular climax of life, but a quality of life in general of these human beings. Yet this subjective religious state of being is not limited to its psychological reality but is itself *metaphysical* and possesses a timeless quality borne solely by the spirituality of these temporal individuals. In the following I will expand on several aspects of this interpretation.

*First,* such an interpretation of the religious soul may be applied appropriately to the soul in general. The rather sentimental sobriquet "painter of the soul," which has long been applied to Rembrandt, is derived from a valid impression, but this impression cannot be appreciated fully unless one takes its opposite into account. Philosophers have been intent on demonstrating the totality of the world and understanding its systematic unity; yet it is a remarkable fact that almost without exception, they show an indifference to—perhaps even a rejection of—psychology. They make frequent reference to the theme of comprehending the very essence of human existence and reaching the point at which God is within our grasp, especially when we fathom the ultimate depths of our own soul; yet surely this very idea is a transplanting of the soul into a metaphysical sphere, a transcending of those specific qualities of the soul which it inherently possesses. And however much one regards the soul as being intertwined with the world—whether one views the soul as the very climax of the world's development or, conversely, the world as being within the soul as the soul's conception and product—wherever the soul lives purely as a soul and is sensed as such, the soul and the world are mutually exclusive. Such mutual exclusion is not denied by these various associations, but is viewed as a hindrance yet to be overcome.

This idea does not apply only to philosophy, but to religions and the arts as well: wherever the totality of existence is to be fixed, symbolized, or dominated in its entire breadth or its objective center, the *soul* loses that particular emphasis which, of all things in the world, can be given to it alone. On the other hand, wherever such emphasis occurs, it offers no path to a sense of controlling or understanding the cosmic order. Precisely because Rembrandt is the "painter of the soul," his figures lack the *cosmic* element that is so hard to define and that can be seen in many of Hodler's figures, for example. They express not their psychological self but some universal value of which they are a part, just as all others are. Buddha figures possess a noncosmic character and a passionately passionless rejection of the world. Yet even they have a very definite—if negative—relationship to the deepest concept of this very world, and this is why they can easily appear "soulless" in the psychological sense. Rembrandt's focusing of all interest onto the soul itself does not allow any such relationship, whether in the subject of his work or in the style of portrayal.

In one painting by Rembrandt, all of this finds positive expression: the *Resurrection* in Munich. In the foreground, the warriors stagger down from the raised tombstone: here we have the chaos of the mortal world in all its senselessness, partly violent, partly ludicrous. Above this is the angel, immersed in immortal radiance as if he had left the door to heaven open and divine glory were pouring out behind him. And now, hardly more than a shadow in the corner, as if far away, the head of Jesus is raised, its expression barely recognizable. Suddenly we realize: this is the *soul,* wan and suffering, deathly stiff, and yet a life source before which both the mortal and the heavenly sphere fade to nothing. No pictorial or mythical-religious emphasis is given to this head; it is quite simply the soul, which as such is not of this world, nor indeed of the other world. It is beyond the awesome irreconcilability of these two opposites, which encompass all other forms of existence and in which heaven and earth are fixed here. Rembrandt painted this picture when he was in his thirties, and it might be viewed as a symbol and a program for his later masterpieces. It demonstrates the uniqueness of the soul, how its existence and its value stand above any other existence or value, in a sovereign sphere of its own—an objective realm of the subjective, which, with regard to the earthly and perhaps the metaphysical cosmos, is not required to integrate or be integrated. Yet only this absoluteness of the principle of the soul can sustain a religiosity whose metaphysical content is not some fixed fact of faith but the religious life of the soul itself.

*Second,* in Rembrandt's art religiosity is just as much part of his subjects as is their vitality, because their being religious is the very quality of their lives. Yet such portrayal still possesses an objectivity and a sense of firm spiritual purpose. In order to appreciate this, we must look at the artist's work from a quite different perspective.

A more searching analysis of art draws a precise distinction between the *portrayal of the religious* and *religious portrayal,* however many works may display a unification of the two. Such a distinction, necessary in all kinds of artistic subjects, tends to be more readily recognized in theory than actually practiced. The poet's or painter's representation of a sensuous scene need not be sensuous in its manner of depiction; its formal character can be purely artistic. Conversely, the artistic portrayal of content that has no appeal in this respect might be invested with a highly stimulating sensual attraction—for example, certain ornaments by Aubrey Beardsley. From this point of view, such art resembles music that, although devoid of any specific content, can evoke or express extreme sensory stimulation. This effect can be described in general as follows: some contents experienced as reality, as in the empirical world, possess certain qualities or colorings that are not an obvious or natural part of those things when transposed into the form of art. Art, too, however, can possess or not possess these qualities in any of its individual manifestations; the artistic form as such can be permeated with such qualities, whether or not the empirical form of the same content displays them. Therefore, the important thing here is to grasp the principle that there can be religious works of art whose subject need not be at all religious (though it also might be that), just as it is recognized more widely that there are thoroughly irreligious works of art that have a religious subject.

This may explain why the captivating feature of Rembrandt's paintings of biblical motifs, which at first sight apparently offer no more than a scene from the milieu of the petty bourgeoisie, can be expressed thus: the act of artistic production itself, the manual application of needle, feather, or brush, is religiously inspired. The dynamics of creation itself possess that unique coloring which we call religious and which in the field of historical faith and in the transcendental sphere crystallizes to form the actual "objects" of religion. For this reason such paintings do not require any religious detail; they are religious in their entirety, because the a priori function that created them is religious. The biblical nature of their themes merely facilitates;

it stimulates the artist to let this function take effect and stimulates the observer to sense it.

The possible effects of the artist's pictorial means might be compared to certain features of *vocal music*. In both the lieder and the operas of many composers there is a complete inner detachment between words and music. Mozart sometimes set music to the most miserable words, in the sure knowledge that the beauty of the music itself was more than enough to compensate for their inferior quality. With Mozart, as with other composers, words and music are a factual unity, though they belong to entirely different orders of meaning. The situation is quite different with Bach, for example, or later particularly with Schumann. Here, there is such a depth of integration of words and music that the former give the impression of being perfectly malleable; the most profound essence of their mood provides the root from which the work of art as a whole can grow. In being determined by the fundamental character of the words, the music channels this quality back into the words. The character of the words is thus purified and reinforced by its musical elaboration and is invested with a new creative power.

When applied to the religious subject and its artistic depiction, the first relationship of words to music mentioned here would be the equivalent of the High Renaissance and Rubens. A Madonna's inner significance is irrelevant to Raphael, and Rubens does not inquire into the subjective meaning of the Descent from the Cross. In both cases, the art of painting is entirely *self-sufficient;* that it contains a subject with its own individual significance, like a foreign body, does not affect our impression of it. With Rembrandt, however, the process of artistic creation is itself permeated with the fundamental religiousness of the scene portrayed; this inner quality becomes a part of the creative process itself. In becoming a work of art, the subject is given a form and a soul such that its essence is identified totally with its artistic portrayal; this essential quality of the artistic function is enriched by the universal meaning of its subject, far transcending its empirical detail.

This interpretation clearly contains the possibility of a subjectivist error that is to be avoided. None of this is intended as a claim that Rembrandt was a religious individual who was able to pour the religious faith of his personal life into the creative products of that life. We do not know his position in this respect; any evidence we have seems to me to weigh more heavily against his being very positively religious. But as a *painter*, in his function as the creator of these paintings, Rembrandt is religious. This again is the distinction between Rembrandt and the other painter of piety, Fra Angelico. Fra Angelico is religious in a personal sense, and of a childlike sincerity. He possesses a directness that one might term naturalism, not in what he painted but in how he painted it. He carries over the attitude of his real life into his artistic work. In Rembrandt's case, however, as far as we can judge, it is not his personal experience but the artistic process, the manner of conception and creation, that gives his works their religious quality. For this reason it cannot be said that his works owe this quality to the realistic observation of religious persons. Of course his figures come across as empirically pious, and, as I described above, their religiousness is drawn from within. Yet beneath this immediate impression there is a deeper level, as a functional a priori: it is what we must call religious painting, as opposed to the painting of religious subjects.

This characteristic religiousness is really no more than an inherent quality of the style of painting, its immanent source — not a reality of life merely expressed in painting. Indeed, not only the figures but the entire paintings display this artistic a priori individually: light and air, the composition and the entire milieu possess this fundamental religiousness, which often cannot be demonstrated in specific details. Such an overall character can be seen only in the work as a whole — that is, in a general stylistic gesture of artistic creation, even though it manifests itself only in a particular thematic area of the artist's work. The religiousness we mentioned above as an inner spiritual source, a quality of the life process of Rembrandt's figures that has no specific content, thus shifts to a deeper level of significance: religiosity becomes an inherent quality of the artistic medium of painting or drawing. It is the solemnity, the blend of dark with light and of the inexpressible with the obvious. The artist's means of expression *is* religious; it does not merely possess religion, whether this is the avowal of actual personal faith, the reproduction of observed religiosity, or the portrayal of the content of religion (though both of the latter also may apply). I know of no creator of religious works of art who has placed the element of religion at this profound level, totally free of all mere realism, as a law shaping the creative process itself and thus visibly "universal and necessary" within the created work.

*Third,* we have considered what is unique about Rembrandt's religious works, as regards both his subjects and the artistic function: it is that religion is captured as a quality of the soul, as *religiosity,* stripped of all traditional dogma and transcendental content; and also that this primarily subjective phenomenon indeed has objective, metaphysical value because, on the one hand, it represents the absoluteness of the soul in the individuals portrayed; on the other hand, this subjectivism has become a priori a factor determining the artistic process, thus possessing the full objectivity of the art form and forming an intrinsic part of the objective process of artistic creation. Rembrandt has one particular means at his disposal, which enables him to make this constellation come true in such a way as to transcend human individuality: it is *light.* In my view one would be quite mistaken to consider the light in his religious works to be symbolic. That may be the case in some of his landscape paintings and etchings: in those works it is intended to bring out certain differentiated moods and therefore might be more correctly termed allegorical than symbolic. In his religious works, however, light immediately generates an atmosphere of religiousness, a coloring of the whole world as religious. It is not a symbol, as in other paintings—for example, in the ray of light beaming down from the opened heavens or in the radiance emanating from the Christ child. It is like the religiousness of Rembrandt's human figures; they bear this quality within themselves, not as the manifestation of some higher transcendental element or item of dogma. This light is religious as a natural reality, as it were, just as the religiousness of Rembrandt's human figures is a spiritual reality. The latter are rustic, narrow-minded and quite earthly; yet their religiosity possesses a metaphysical grandeur and is a metaphysical fact. Rembrandt's light in his religious etchings and paintings is something of a very palpable, earthly nature. It does not demonstrate some higher principle, and yet it transcends the empirical; it is the metaphysical transfiguration of concrete being. It does not raise mortal existence to a higher order but portrays it in such a way that it actually *is* a higher order itself when viewed with religious eyes.

It is not pantheism that is being described here, because this can barely be expressed in the plastic arts: such art forms can suggest a pantheistic atmosphere only as some distant mood hovering far above, perhaps as in the ancient art of eastern Asia. Pantheism is either the reconciliation of a dualism whose traces are not entirely erased—and cannot be erased if the new-found unity is to be conveyed fully—or else an open or hidden rejection of sensory reality in favor of the sole reality of the transcendental sphere. Both of these are quite alien to Rembrandt's approach. His particular light emanates neither from the sun nor from some artificial source but from his artistic imagination, and yet it is of a totally spiritual and sensory character. Its stature and its otherworldliness are thoroughly earthly features that one might describe as deriving from artistic experience.

There is an interesting analogy with historical facts here. If one considers the Dutch people as they are portrayed as rustics and burghers—full of the joy of living, their feet firmly on the ground, taking sincere pleasure in good food and drink—it is surely most devastating to consider that these very people were unreservedly prepared to suffer death and worse for their ideals, for their political and religious freedom. And this almost seems to be symbolized in many of Rembrandt's religious paintings and etchings: simple figures, devoid of any subjective fantasy, unrefined, and down-to-earth, and yet possessing within them this inherent religious quality. They are now engulfed once more in light so that they can embody an absoluteness that is pure inner transfiguration, earthly and immortal at once, yet not out-reaching itself. Works such as *Rest on the Flight to Egypt* in the museum of The Hague, or the tint drawing *The Good Samaritan* in Berlin, are unique in the history of artistic expression. Just as the music of a great composer surpasses the specific, expressible content of the words of the song, thus expressing the ultimate meaning of the song as a pure, unblemished whole, so it is in these works, with each particularity of the almost unrecogniz-able figures: each specific detail of the scene is integrated com-pletely into the drama of light and shade, a drama that moves us deeply both as a vision and as the most universal, metaphysical, and spiritual interpretation of the scene.

The idea of *"generality,"* which we may contrast with any concept of specific individuality, can be gained from very dif-ferent perspectives. The conception, the sensory impression, the emotional value, the content alone, or the form alone—any of these may be singled out in any individual manifestation of life as its universal element, individualized by the various other fea-tures that give it its unique overall character. In these works of Rembrandt in which the light is so central, the religious mood provides the general element on which the whole scene is based, the transcendence of what is portrayed visually, its inherent grandeur and awesomeness. Light is the most general element of the visually portrayable world because it is light alone that makes vision possible; its pure modifications therefore might be taken as the most profound transcendental plan for any optical scene. It is also the general element of a particular picture, beyond any higher significance—just as the music is the universal element of the words of the song, or rather of the whole song in its final form as an integrated work of art. The unique achievement of Rembrandt's art is that he has captured the religious mood and sense of grandeur as the general element of his works, with light as the visual agent of this generality.

Here we have the most uncompromising rejection of any dogmatic content. If a biblical scene is the actual subject of a painting, it will remain part of an objective sacred tradition even if the human figures are depicted in such a way that their traditional religious meaning is swallowed up by the autonomous meaning of subjective religious spirituality. But even this idea ceases to apply where light is no longer there simply to illuminate the scene but is itself the subject of the painting, the self-sufficient dynamic, the depth and irreconcilability to which the human, biblical scene is incidental, as it were. We have seen that the individual figures express the existence of the soul as a religious phenomenon — pure *piety* transcending all dogma, or indeed forming its very basis. In the same way, the whole scene in its historical and dogmatic immutability is now reduced to that which is most general within it: the light. It is as if the light were to reveal the general mood of some universal soul whose religiosity permeated this part of our world, a religiosity whose exaltation and repose, awe and bliss, transcended this and any other confessional content, because it is the central, general element at the very core of any such content.

I do not intend to give the impression that Rembrandt was the only artist to have created truly religious paintings. On the contrary, we can appreciate the uniqueness of his art only if we consider the claims of the converse form of religious art: that is, *objective religious art,* which is based on the existence of religious facts and values external to the individual soul. I outlined the differences between the two types at the beginning of this essay; it will suffice simply to show a number of limitations imposed on the religiosity of the individual soul and on its artistic expression, because the soul is restricted to itself and lives its religious life entirely inwardly, without any conscious reference to a transcendental sphere. The art of an objective religion invests the holy figures and events with their own specific importance, liberated from any random spiritual reflexes, but this is not all. Particularly significant are precisely the subjective processes within the religious soul that are caused by the emphasis given to the transcendental sphere, the objective facts of faith. Of course, Rembrandt's religious men and women are filled with the anticipation, certainty, and emotion that are of divine provenance. For them, however, this separate transcendental sphere is not of primary importance, it is not the essence of their religiousness, so to speak. Their crucial source remains that which flows from within the soul itself; its essential inner life is its religious destiny. For this reason, even the domain of spiritual experience in Rembrandt's religious works displays obvious gaps.

To begin with, one essential Christian motif is lacking, that of *hope*. This emotion clearly can come to full fruition only in positive reference to some sphere that transcends the soul. Above all the figures of the Trecento hovers Dante's Paradise; in the eccentric movements of the Baroque, man literally thrusts himself upward to heaven. Not so in Rembrandt; with him there is neither hope nor hopelessness. His figures are beyond this category; the soul has withdrawn from the extremes of heaven and hell and has taken refuge more directly in itself. There are two further religious experiences that we do not find in Rembrandt's figures: the need for salvation and the need for divine mercy. Even though these spiritual states may be created by forces within the soul, such states gain their specific character only in the conscious envisagement of something external to the soul, a source of spiritual dependence.

This point touches on an aspect of human behavior that has a very broad significance. In psychological terms, we may be convinced that all we have is our own consciousness, and that the content of our lives is simply a modification of self-consciousness. Metaphysically speaking, we may believe that all our experience and learning is the path of the soul toward itself, and that the soul can never find anything new that was not already its own. Yet in many instances, this inner development is by no means direct; it requires some external point of reference. For the soul can reach its highest goal—though admittedly this always lies within itself—only by a bypath recognized as external. This new development is no doubt related to the fact that life has a characteristic tendency to go beyond itself, as it were, reaching out beyond itself at every moment. Such a tendency can be seen in mankind's instinct for survival, for example, in his urge to procreate, or in his power of imagination and will. This striving beyond itself or stepping outside itself is then reversed, so to speak; life, having followed the path that directs it toward external and ideational objectivity, returns to itself once more. It has gained personal possessions and reactions that are now its own, but it could gain or create them only by taking this step outside itself. Supposing that in all of this the soul were in fact circling within itself, this striving beyond its own boundaries or creation of a distinct other or opposite to react to would be the nature of its inner life.

Certainly some kinds of spiritual fulfillment remain entirely within the boundaries of the soul: qualities of existence, of emotion, of inner development or struggle. Rembrandt's religiosity finds expression within the sphere and purpose of such qualities. But even if one were to assume that all religion consisted only of this *self-centered* spiritual life—and that all objectivity external to the soul were merely a myth, a mirroring, a hypostatization, or whatever—it is still an undeniable fact that certain purely inner experiences can occur only where this atmosphere of immanence is pierced, and that the soul lives by relating to objective, external phenomena, pursuing its centrifugal course by way of this detour outside itself. Even though the capacity to believe is determined by the soul itself, "faith" is possible only by this detour. This is the only way in which hope and despair, salvation and mercy in turn find religious expression. This is so even

though, from a nonreligious perspective such as the purely intellectual, that with which the soul interacts to achieve this detour
appears as an artifact of itself. For this reason, such religiosity
lacks the element of *peril*. All the terrible uncertainties, the sense
of being at the mercy of a higher power, of groping in the
dark — all of this is absent here. There is no sense of risk from the
absolute obligation imposed by a transcendental power, such as
that which tore apart Michelangelo's life and was transposed in
many different forms into the lives of his figures. This is not to
accuse Rembrandt's figures of having some bourgeois sense of
security: they are simply beyond this alternative between peril
and redemption because both of these — along with all the other
elements of the order defined by these extremes — are made possible only by shifting the religious emphasis onto the objective
content of faith. If this emphasis rests on the subjective process
of religion — however metaphysical and absolute it may be — and
if religiousness in its most profound sense is not based on the coexistence of subject and object, then the requirement for these
emotions is lacking. For this reason, it is not merely a weakness
of Rembrandt's art that they are not represented there; it is the
necessary and affirmative consequence of the very nature of his
art, which stands with unique strength and stature in direct antithesis to the artistic forms of objective religion.

**PART 4**   *Methods in the Study of Religion*

# NINE  *A Contribution to the Sociology of Religion [1898]*

No light will ever be cast in the sybillic twilight that, for us, surrounds the origin and nature of religion as long as we insist on approaching it as a single problem requiring only a single word for its solution. Thus far no one has been able to offer a definition of religion that is both precise and sufficiently comprehensive. No one has been able to grasp its ultimate essence, shared by the religions of Christians and of South Sea islanders, of Buddha and Vitzliputzli. We have as yet no definition that distinguishes religion clearly from mere metaphysical speculation or from belief in ghosts. As a consequence, not even the purest and highest manifestations of religion can claim exemption from examination for the presence of such contaminations. The multiplicity of psychological motives ascribed to religion corresponds to this ill-defined conception of its nature. It does not matter whether fear or love, ancestor worship or self-deification, the moral instincts or the feeling of dependence are regarded as the root of religion; each one of these theories is entirely erroneous only when it is assumed to be the sole explanation, but is justified when it claims to point out merely one of the sources of religion.

Hence the solution to the problem will depend on the following preconditions. First, all the impulses, ideas, and conditions operating in this domain must be inventoried. Then it must be determined clearly that the significance of known particular motives may not be expanded arbitrarily into general laws that supposedly govern the essence of anything religious. But this is not the only qualification that must be made in an attempt to clarify the religious significance of the phenomena of social life, which themselves are entirely unrelated to religion.

In addition, we must insist that no matter how mundanely and how empirically the origin of ideas about the supramundane and the transcendent is explained, neither the subjective, emotional value of these ideas nor their objective value as matters of fact is at all in question. Both these values lie beyond the limits that our merely causal, psychological inquiry aims to reach.

If we try accordingly to find the beginnings of the fundamentally religious in human relations that in themselves are not yet religion, we merely follow a method that has been accepted for some time. It has long been admitted that scholarship is merely a heightening, a reassembling, a refinement of those means of knowledge which, in lesser and dimmer degree, help us to form our judgments and experiences in daily, practical life. We arrive at a genetic explanation of art only when we have analyzed the aesthetic experiences of life—in speech, in the emotions, in business, in social affairs—that are not in themselves artistic. All high and pure forms existed at first experimentally, as it were, in the germ, in connection with other forms; but in order to comprehend them in their highest and independent forms, we must look for them in their undeveloped states. A psychological interpretation of these forms will depend on finding their place in a chain whose links merge and take each other's places, as if by gradual development. By way of an apparently organic growth, this process takes them through a variety of stages, so that the new and the differentiated appear as the growth of the germs. Thus it may help us to achieve an insight into the origin and nature of religion if we can discover in all kinds of nonreligious relationships and intentions certain religious qualities that, as they become independent and self-sufficient, come to be "religion." I do not believe that religious feelings and impulses manifest themselves only in religion; rather, they are to be found in many connections, a contributing factor in various situations. Only with extreme intensity and specificity does religion appear as an independent sector of life, as an area with boundaries of its own. Now, in order to find the fragments of religion in the making in the midst of human interactions—or, as it were, in order to discover religion before it becomes religion—we must digress to what seem at first to be entirely unrelated phenomena.

It has long been known that custom is the chief form of social control in the less developed cultures. Those life conditions which on the one hand are subsequently codified as laws and enforced by the state and, on the other hand, are subjected to the free consent of the cultivated and trained individual are, in narrower and more primitive circles, guaranteed by that peculiar, immediate control of the individual by his environment which we call custom. Custom, law, and voluntary morality, although different unifying elements of social life, nonetheless can carry the same obligations and content—indeed, this has been the case among different peoples at different times.[1] Many of the norms and practices of public life are supported both by the free play of competing forces and by the control of lower elements by higher. Many social interests were at first protected by the family organization; but later, or in other places, they were brought under the care of purely occupational associations[2] or of the state. Generally it can be asserted that the interrelations that characterize the life of society are always due to definite ends, causes, and interests. As long as these persist, representing as it were the matter of social life, the forms in which they express themselves may be exceedingly diverse, just as the same form and type of interaction may have the most varied content. It seems to me that among these forms which human relations assume, and which may have the most diverse content, there is one that

[1] These functional differences may of course be very highly significant: Socrates had to die because of them, since he wanted to transform into reality through the freely judging conscience of the individual the same ethical principles that the ancient Greek tradition protected by means of strict customs and conventions [footnote by Simmel].

[2] Compare Durkheim 1893.

can be described only as religious, although of course this desig-
nation anticipates the name of the mature phenomenon for its
mere beginning and preconditions. Yet the coloring that justifies
this description must not be seen as a mere reflection of an existing religion. Rather, human contact, in the purely psychological
aspect of its interaction, develops that definite tone which, when
heightened to an independent substance, is known as religion.

We can see, for example, that many human relationships
harbor a religious element. The relationship of a devoted child
to his parent, of an enthusiastic patriot to his country, of the fervent cosmopolite to humanity; the relationship of the worker
to his insurgent class or of the proud feudal lord to his fellow nobles; the relationship of the subject to his ruler or of the
true soldier to his army—all these relationships, with their infinite variety of content, can be seen to share a psychological
form. This form has a common tone that can be described only
as religious. All religiosity contains a peculiar admixture of unselfish surrender and fervent desire, of humility and exaltation,
of sensual concreteness and spiritual abstraction; this occasions
a certain degree of emotional tension, a specific ardor and certainty of the subjective conditions, an inclusion of the subject
in a higher order—an order which, at the same time, is felt to
be something inward and personal. This religious quality is contained, it seems to me, in many other relationships, and gives
them a tone that distinguishes them from relationships based on
pure egoism, pure influence, or even purely moral forces. Obviously this quality is present with more or less strength, sometimes appearing merely as a light overtone and at other times as
quite a distinct color. In many important instances, the development period of the relationships is characterized in this way;
that is, the content that was borne by other forms of human relationships at one period assumes a religious form in other periods. This is illustrated best by those laws which at some times or
in some places reveal a theocratic character and are completely

under religious sanctions, but which at other times and places are guaranteed either by the state or by custom.

It would even seem as if the indispensable requirements of society have frequently emerged from an entirely undifferentiated form in which moral, religious, and juridical sanctions were still mingled indiscriminately, such as the *dharma* of the Hindus, the *themis* of the Greeks, and the *fas* of the Romans. Then, as historical conditions varied, now one and now the other of these evolving forms developed into the agent of such requirements. In the relationship of the individual to the group, these changes also can be observed. In times when patriotism is aroused, this relationship assumes a devotion, a fervor, and a readiness of self-surrender that can be described only as religious; at other times it is controlled by convention or by law. For us, the important thing is that in every case it is a question of human relations. It is merely a change, as it were, in the shape of these relations when the merely conventional transmutes into the religious and the religious transmutes into the legal, and then the legal transmutes into voluntary morality. As a matter of fact, many socially injurious immoralities first found a place in the criminal code because they were punished by the church; or, as illustrated by anti-Semitism, a socioeconomic or racial relationship between certain subdivisions within a group can be elevated to the religious category, yet without really ceasing to be a social relationship; or, as it is assumed, cults of prostitution really were a religious form of sexual life which earlier or elsewhere was controlled by pure convention.

In view of these examples, we must now deal in more detail with a misunderstanding already referred to above. The theory set forth here is not intended to prove that certain social interests and occurrences are controlled by a religious system that already exists independently. That certainly occurs often enough, bringing about combinations of the greatest historical importance — and indeed being very significant in the examples cited. What

I mean, however, is precisely the reverse connection, although admittedly much less apparent and more difficult to distinguish. In those social relations the coloring that we call religious, on account of its analogy with existing religiosity, comes into being spontaneously, as a purely social psychological constellation, one of the possible forms of conduct between person and person. By contrast, religion conceived as an independent phenomenon is a derivative thing, almost like the state in the ancient Roman or the modern sense. The latter, as an objective and self-sufficient entity, is secondary to the original relations and rules that palpably governed interacting individuals. Only gradually are the conservation and execution of these relations and rules projected onto institutional spheres such as the state. The entire history of social life is permeated by this process: the immediate interdetermination among individuals with which their social life begins emerges into separate and independent organisms. Thus, from the types of conduct necessary for preserving group life there arises on the one hand the law that codifies them and on the other the judge whose business it is to specialize in applying them. Thus, as another example, socially necessary labors are first performed with everyone's cooperation and according to the crude empiricism of daily life. From these labors there develops on the one hand a technology as a theoretical system of knowledge and rules and on the other hand a laboring class assigned the task of applying this technology. In a similar manner—although in these infinitely complex things the analogy is always embroidered with innumerable deviations—this transformation may occur with religion.

The individual in a group is related to others, or to everyone, in the way described above; that is, his relations with them are characterized by a certain degree of exaltation, devotion, fervency, and inwardness. From this there develops a theoretical content: gods who protect these relations, who appear to have stimulated the emotions, and who, by their very existence, then bring into sharp relief—as an independent entity, so to speak — what had existed previously only as a form of human relationship more or less blended with everyday life. This complex of ideas or images gains in the priesthood an executive or specialized occupational channel, much as law is executed by the judiciary or the pursuit of knowledge by academics. When this separation and materialization of religion has been accomplished, religion in turn reflects on the immediate psychic relations among people, giving them the now recognized coloring of so-called religiosity. In doing so, however, it merely gives back what it received originally. And perhaps it may be asserted that often wondrous and abstruse religious ideas never could have obtained their power over men if they had not been the formulas for or embodiments of previously existing relations for which consciousness merely had not yet found a more appropriate expression.

The intellectual motif underlying this discussion is very general and may be expressed as a comprehensive rule, of which the materialistic conception of history is a single illustration. When materialism derives the entire *content* of historic life from the *form* of the economy and defines custom and law, art and religion, science and social structure accordingly, a part of a very comprehensive process is mistaken for the whole. The development of the forms and contents of social life, throughout its wide territory and its multiplicity of phenomena, is such that the selfsame content finds expression in various forms, and the same form can have a variety of contents. The events of history arrange themselves *as if* they were controlled by a tendency to sustain as much as possible every sum of moving energies. This is clearly why history does not disintegrate into a collection of incoherent moving forces but intimately binds together the synchronous as well as the successive.[3]

Any particular form of life — social, literary, religious, per-

---

[3] Compare the chapter "Historical Materialism" in Simmel 1977, 185–200.

sonal—can outlive its connection with a single kind of content, and can also lend itself unchanged to a new one, and a single kind of content can retain its essential nature through a wealth of successive forms—and it is precisely this that maintains the continuity of history. It prevents the occurrence at some point of an irrational leap, a break in the connection with the entire past. Because the evolution of the race generally advances from the sensual and external to the mental and internal—only, it is true, to reverse this order frequently—this transmutation toward the form of the abstract and the intellectual occurs commonly even in economic life. Thus forms that have their origin in economic interests will expand into entirely different aspects of life. Yet that is only *one* of the instances in which continuity and the principle of parsimony are found in history. When, for example, the form of government exhibited in the state is repeated in the family; when the prevailing religion gives direction and inspiration to art; when frequent wars make the individual brutal and aggressive even in peace; when political divisions influence nonpolitical affairs and align diverging tendencies of culture according to party principles—these are all expressions of this peculiar character of all historic life, of which the materialistic theory of history illuminates only a single side. And it is precisely this character that illustrates the development with which we are concerned here—how forms of social relations either condense or refine themselves into a system of religious ideas or add new elements to existing ideas. Viewed differently, a specific kind of emotional content that arose in the form of individual interaction transmutes itself in this relationship into a transcendent idea. It becomes a new category in which both forms and contents take on new life, although originating in human relationships. I shall test the utility of this general notion by applying it to a number of specific aspects of religious life.

The faith that has come to be regarded as the essence and substance of religion is first of all a relationship *between human beings;* for this relationship is a matter of *practical* faith and by no means merely a lower form, or attenuation, of theoretical belief. When I say "I believe in God," the assertion means something entirely different from the statement "I believe that light is diffused through ether" or "The moon is inhabited" or "Human nature is immutable." It not only means that I accept the existence of God even though it is not fully demonstrable, but also implies a certain spiritual relationship to Him, a surrendering of affections to Him, an orientation of life toward Him. In all this there is a peculiar mixture of faith as a way of "knowing" with practical impulses and emotional feelings. This faith has an analogy in how humans become part of society: we do not by any means base our mutual relations on what we know conclusively about each other. Rather, our feelings and impressions articulate themselves in certain representations that can be described only as matters of faith; these, in turn, have an effect on practical conditions. We illustrate a specific psychological reality, hard to define, when we "believe in someone"—the child in its parents, the subordinate in his superior, the friend in a friend, the individual in the people, the subject in his sovereign. The social role of this faith has never been investigated, but this much is certain: without it, society would disintegrate. Obedience, for example, is largely based on it.[4] In innumerable instances obedience depends neither on the certain knowledge of law and superiority nor on mere affection or influence, but on that intermediate psychic complex we call faith in a person or a group of persons.

It has often been thought incomprehensible that individuals, and entire classes, allow themselves to be oppressed and exploited, even though potentially they possess ample power to secure liberation. But this is precisely the result of a benign, uncritical *faith* in the power, merits, superiority, and goodness of those in authority—a faith that is by no means an uncertain,

[4] Compare Max Weber's typology of *Herrschaft* (domination) in Weber 1978, 212–301.

theoretical assumption but a complex compounded of knowledge, instinct, and feeling, which is described uniformly and simply as faith. That we still can retain our faith in an individual in the face of reasonable contradictory evidence or appearance, no matter how obvious, is one of the strongest of the ties that bind human society. Now, this faith is certainly religious in character. I do not mean that religion existed first, and that sociological conditions borrowed their attributes from it. Rather I believe that these social ties, irrespective of the religious data, arise as a purely interindividual, psychological relationship, which later exhibits itself abstractly in religious faith. In the faith in something divine, the pure process of faith has become incorporate, so to speak; it has separated itself from its social counterpart. From the subjective faith process there develops, conversely, an object for that faith. The faith in human relations that originates time and again as a social necessity now becomes an independent, typical function of humanity that authenticates itself spontaneously from within.

Similarly, it is not rare for a certain object to produce a certain psychic process in us, and subsequently for this process, having become independent, to create a corresponding object for itself. Human intercourse, in both its ordinary and its highest content, depends in so many ways on the psychological form of faith that the need for "believing" develops from it. In doing so it creates objects for its justification, much as the impulses of love or veneration can fasten onto objects that in themselves could by no means evoke such sentiments but that instead reflect the subject's needs. Viewed from the other side, God as creator has been described as the product of the human need for causal explanations. This assertion certainly does not deny the concept of God its objective reality, nor does it deny that there is a reality that corresponds to this concept; only the motive from which it grew into an idea is in question. Let us assume that the infinitely frequent application of the causal idea, having its origin in the mundane world, finally made dominant the need for causal explanation. This need, normally denied in the realm of the absolute, was fulfilled in the idea of an Absolute Being as the cause of the world. A similar process may transmute faith beyond the confines of its social origins, develop it into something almost like a physical need, and beget for it the idea of the divine as an absolute object.

A second aspect of social life that develops into a corresponding aspect of religious life is found in the concept of *unity*. We do not simply accept our disconnected and manifold impressions of things but look instead for the connections and relations that bind them into a unity. We presuppose everywhere the presence of higher unities and centers for seemingly separate phenomena, so that we can orient ourselves amid the confusion in which they come to us. That human inclination is assuredly something that has grown out of social realities and necessities. Directly and appreciably, particularly in the clan, in the family, in the state, in every voluntary association, we find a whole made up of separate elements, which nevertheless is effectively controlled by the center. When primitive organizations so often are found organized by tens,[5] it means clearly that the group relationship is similar to that of the fingers of the hand—relative freedom and independent movement of the individual and, at the same time, unity of purpose and inseparableness of existence from others. That all social life is interaction makes it at once become a unity; what does unity signify, but that many are mutually related, and that the fate of each is felt by all? That this unity of society is occasionally attacked, that the freedom of the individual prompts him to break away from it, and that even in the closest and most naive ties unity is not as obviously dominant as in the constituent parts of an organism—all of this must have made it grow within human consciousness as a special form and a special value of existence.

[5] Note that the dean (Latin: *decanus*) was originally the spokesperson for a group of ten.

The unity of things and interests with which we first become acquainted in the social realm finds its highest representation — and one separated, as it were, from all material considerations — in the idea of the divine; it occurs most completely, of course, in the monotheistic religions, but to a certain extent also in the lower religions. The deepest significance of the idea of God is that the manifoldness and the contradictoriness of things find in it their coherence and unity — whether the absolute unity of the one God or the partial unities of polytheism pertaining to particular provinces of reality. Thus, for example, the social life of the ancient Arabs, with the all-controlling influence of the tribal unit, foreshadowed monotheism. Among Semitic peoples such as the Jews, the Phoenicians, and the Canaanites, their way of maintaining uniformity and its transformations was reflected clearly in the character of their divine principle: as long as the family unit was the prevailing form, Baal signified only a father, whose children were the people. But when the social aggregate included foreign branches not related by blood, Baal then became a ruler objectively enthroned above. As soon as *social* unity loses the character of blood relationship, religious unity also loses it, so that the latter appears as the pure, detached form of the former.

Even the unification that bridges gender differentiation creates a particular religious type. An important factor in the social life of the Syrians, Assyrians, and Lydians was the psychological blurring of gender differences. This finds expression in deities who combine such different features within themselves: the half-male Astarte, the male-female Sandon, the sun god Melkarth, who exchanges gender symbols with the moon goddess. This is not merely an illustration of the trivial idea that man projects himself into his gods — a general truth that requires no proof. The question is rather to find the particular human characteristics whose development and extension beyond the human dimension create gods. One must also bear in mind that the gods do not exist as the idealization of individual characteristics, or of the power, the moral or immoral character traits, or the in-clinations and needs of individuals; rather, the interindividual forms of life often give their content to religious ideas. When certain phases and intensities of social functions assume their purest, most abstract, and at the same time incarnate forms, they become the objects of religions. Thus it can be said that religion, whatever else it may be, consists of forms of social relationships that, when separated from their empirical content, become in-dependent and are projected on substances of their own.

Two further considerations will illustrate how much the *unity* of the group belongs to the functions that have devel-oped religious significance. Particularly in primitive periods, the unity of the group is based on and indicated by the absence of either fighting or competition within the group, in contrast to the relationships sustained with all outsiders. Probably, there is no other single domain in which this noncompetitive form of existence, this identity of aim and interest, is represented so clearly and completely as in religion. The peaceful character of group life just mentioned is only relative. Most of the efforts put forth within the group imply an attempt to exclude others from the same goal; to reduce as much as possible the disproportion between desire and satisfaction, even at the expense of others; at least to find a reason for doing and enjoying by distinguishing oneself from others. It is almost solely in religion that individu-als' energies can find the fullest development without coming into competition with each other, because, as it is so aptly ex-pressed by Jesus, there is room for all in God's house. Although the goal is common to all, it is possible for all to achieve it, not only without mutual exclusion but through mutual coopera-tion. One might consider the profound way in which Holy Communion expresses that the same goal exists for all and is to be reached by the same means; or indeed the feasts that help to become most visible the union of those who are moved by the same religious emotions—from the rude feasts of primitive reli-gions, in which merging into a union finally climaxes in sexual orgies, to that purest expression of the *pax hominibus,* which extends far beyond any single group. The absence of competition that conditions unity as the life form of the group—but that always reigns only relatively and partially in the group—finds its absolute and most intense realization in the religious realm.

It might actually be said of religion, as of faith, that it represents in substance that which regulates the group life in form and function—indeed, to a certain extent, consists of the materialization of that quality. This quality in turn assumes a personal form in a priesthood that, despite its historic connection with certain classes, is fundamentally above *all* individuals. Precisely on that account the priesthood represents the focus and the unity of the ideal life content for all. Thus the celibacy of Catholic priests frees them from every *particular* relationship to any element or group of elements and makes possible a uniform relationship to each, just as "society" or the "state" stands above individuals as the abstract unity that represents all their relationships. To cite a thoroughly concrete instance, throughout the Middle Ages the church provided every benevolent impulse with the great convenience of a central reservoir into which every benefaction could flow unchallenged. He who wished to rid himself of his wealth for the benefit of others did not have to bother about the ways and means, because there existed for this very purpose a universal central organ between the giver and the needy. Thus benevolence, a form of social relationship within the group, was secured in the Church, an organization and unity above the individual.

The attitude toward "heretics" might be described as the reverse of this relationship, though it is based on the same fundamental impulse. That which arrays great masses of people in hatred and moral condemnation of heretics is certainly not the difference in the dogmatic content of teaching; in most instances, this content really is not understood at all. Rather, it is the fact of the *opposition* of the one against the many. The persecution of heretics and dissenters springs from the instinct for the necessity of group unity. It is especially significant that many instances of this kind of religious *deviance* coexist with the unity of the group in all vital matters. But in religion the social instinct for unity has assumed such a pure, abstract, and at the same time substantial form that it no longer requires a union with real interests. Nonconformity therefore seems to threaten the unity—that is to say, the very life form—of the group as it is and as people visualize it. Just as an attack on a palladium or other symbol of group unity will evoke the most violent reaction, even though it may have no direct connection with group unity, so religion is the purest form of unity in society, raised high above all concrete individualities. This truth is demonstrated by the energy with which every heresy, no matter how irrelevant, is combated.

Finally, those internal relations between the individual and the group which we characterize as moral offer such deep analogies to the individual's relationship to his God that they would seem almost to be nothing more than the condensation and transformation of those relations. The whole mysterious richness of those relations is reflected in the many ways in which we "sense" the divine. The compelling and punitive gods, the loving God, the God of Spinoza who cannot return our love, the God who gives or takes away both the directive to act and the strength to follow it—these are precisely the signs through which the ethical relationship between the group and its members unfolds its energies and oppositions. One might consider the feeling of dependence that has been regarded as the essence of all religion. The individual feels himself bound to a universal, to something higher, from which he came and into which he will return, from which he differs and to which he is nonetheless identical. All of these emotions, which meet as in a focal point in the idea of God, can be traced back to the relationship that the individual sustains with the species: on the one hand, with past generations, which supplied him with the principal forms and contents of his being; on the other, with his contemporaries, who condition the manner and extent of his development. If the theory is correct that asserts that all religion is derived from ancestor worship, from the worship and reconciliation of the immortal soul of a forebear, especially a hero and leader, it may confirm this connection; for we are, as a matter of fact, dependent on what was before us, and on what was concentrated most directly in the fathers' authority over their descendants. The deification of ancestors, especially of the ablest and most successful, is as it were the most appropriate expression of the individual's dependence on the previous life of the group, even though the consciousness of the people may reveal other motives for this deification. Thus the humility with which the pious person acknowledges that all that he is and has comes from God, and recognizes in Him the source of his existence and strength, is properly traced to the relationship of the individual to the whole.[6] For man is not absolutely nothing in contrast to God, but only a speck of dust; a weak, but not entirely vain, force; a vessel, yet adapted to receive its contents.

It is the essence of an elucidated idea of God that it becomes the origin and at the same time the unity of all the varieties of being and willing, of all the antitheses and differences, especially of our innermost life interests. Therefore, without more ado we can put the social totality into its place; for from this totality flow all those impulses which come to us as the result of shifting adaptations, all that multiplicity of relationships in which we find ourselves, that development of the organs with which we apprehend the different and almost irreconcilable aspects of the world. And yet the social group is sufficiently unified to be regarded as the real unifying focus of these divergent radiations. Furthermore, the divine origin of kings is merely an expression for the complete concentration of power in their hands; as soon as social unification, the objectification of the whole as against

[6] Compare Durkheim's notion (1893) of the individual's dependence on society.

a part, has reached a certain point, the individual conceives it as a supramundane power. And then, whether he still conceives it directly as social or whether it is already clothed with divinity, the problem arises how much he, as an individual, can and must do to fulfill his destiny, and how much that supramundane principle will assist him. The individual's independence in relation to that power, from which he received his independence and which conditions its aims and methods, is as much a question in this case as in the other. Thus Augustine places the individual within a historic development against which he is as impotent as he is against God. Also, the doctrine of synergism is found throughout the history of the church, as throughout the history of internal politics which it determines. Just as— according to the strict religious conception—the individual is merely a vessel of the grace or wrath of God, so—according to the socialist conception—he is a vessel of the forces emanating from the general public. Both instances reproduce the same fundamental ethical problem concerning the nature and the rights of the individual; in both forms the surrender to the transcending principle frequently offers the only satisfaction still possible when an individuality, thrown wholly on its own resources, no longer has the power to maintain itself.[7]

Assigning such a rank to religious and ethical-social ideas is supported by the conception of God as the personification of those virtues which He Himself demands from the people. He *is* goodness, justice, patience, and so on, rather than as the *possessor* of these attributes; He is, as it is sometimes expressed, perfection in substance; He is goodness itself, love itself, and so on. Morality, the set of imperatives that control interpersonal conduct, has become, so to speak, an everlasting form in Him. Just as practical belief is a relationship between persons that fashions an absolute over and above the form of the relationship; just as

[7] I refer to my book *"Einleitung in die Moralwissenschaft"* (Introduction to the science of morals), vol. 1 [footnote by Simmel].

unity is a form of relationship between a group of persons that raises itself to that personification of the unity of things which appears as the divine; so morality contains those forms of relationship between person and person which group interest has sanctioned. Accordingly, the God who in absolute form represents the relative contents on the one hand embodies the claims and benefits of the group as against those of the individual and on the other hand mandates the ethical-social duties that the individual must perform, divesting them of their relativity, and presents them in Himself in an absolutely substantial form. The relations of persons to each other, which have emerged from the most varied interests, which have been supported by the most strongly opposing forces, and which have been cast in the most diverse forms, also attain a condition whose objectification and relationship to a Being beyond them we call religion. That is, they become both abstract and concrete, a dual development that gives religion the strength with which again, reflexively, it influences those relations. The old idea that God is the Absolute, while that which is human is relative here assumes a new meaning: it is the relations between people that find their substantial and ideal expression in the idea of the divine.

Analyses like this, which touch on the fundamentals of a worldview, are usually accompanied by the hope that their significance will be applied to a wide range of fields, but here the reverse must be the case. Our concern must be that the arguments set forth here not be permitted to intrude beyond their own limited boundaries on neighboring domains. They are not intended to describe the historical course of the creation of religion, but only to point out one of its many sources, quite irrespective of whether this source, in conjunction with others — including those from the domain of the nonreligious — gave birth to religion. Likewise, whether religion had already come into being when the sources discussed here added their contribution to its content depends on the particular historical occasion. In addition, one must bear in mind that religion, as a spiritual ex-

perience, is not a finished product but a vital process that each
soul must create for itself, no matter how stable the traditional
content may be. It is precisely here that the power and the depth
of religion are found—namely, in its persistent ability to draw
a given item of religious data into the flow of the emotions,
whose movements must renew it constantly, like the perpetually
changing drops of water that beget the stable image of the rain-
bow. Therein lie the strength and depth of religion. Hence the
explanation of the source of religion must embrace not only the
historical origin of its tradition, but also its ever-present energies, which allow us to acquire and ultimately possess whatever
religious treasures have come down to us from our fathers. In
this sense there are really "origins" of religion, whose appearance and effectiveness occur long after the "origin" of religion.

Yet even beyond denying that what we offer here is a theory
of the historical origin of religion, it is important to insist that
the objective truth of religion has nothing whatever to do with
this investigation. Even if we have succeeded in the attempt
to understand religion as a product of the inner conditions
of human life, we have not touched at all on the problem of
whether the objective reality lying outside human thought contains the counterpart and the confirmation of the psychic reality
that we have discussed here. Thus the psychology of cognition
seeks to explain how the mind conceives the world to be spatial
and of three dimensions, but it is content to have other inquiries
undertake to prove whether, beyond our mental world, there is
a world of things in themselves of like forms. There may truly
be a limit beyond which the explanation of subjective facts from
purely subjective conditions may prove insufficient. The chain
of causes may have to end somewhere in an objective reality, but
this possibility or necessity can concern only the person who
has in view the complete elucidation of the origin and nature
of religion. It does not affect our attempts to trace only one of
the beams that are focused on religion.

Finally, the most important consideration remains: the

emotional value of religion—that is to say, the innermost re-flexive effect of the ideas of the divine—is entirely independent of all assumptions about the manner in which these ideas originated. Here we touch on the most serious misconception to which the attempt to trace ideal values historically and psychologically is exposed. There are still many people who feel that an ideal is deprived of its greatest charm, that the dignity of an emotion is degraded, if its origin can no longer be regarded as an incomprehensible miracle, a creation from nothing—as if understanding the development of something would affect its value, as if lowliness of origin could challenge the loftiness of the goal already achieved, and as if the dull simplicity of its several elements could destroy the importance of a product that consists of the coordination of the forms and fabric of these elements. Such is the foolish and confused notion that the dignity of humanity is profaned by tracing humankind's origin to the lower animals, as if that dignity did not depend on what man really *is,* no matter what his origin. Persons entertaining such notions will always resist the attempt to understand religion on the basis of elements that in themselves are not yet religious. But precisely such persons who hope to preserve the dignity of religion by denying its historical-psychological origin must be reproached with weakness of religious consciousness. The subjective certainty and emotional depth of such religiousness surely must be limited if the knowledge of its origin and development endangers or even makes the slightest difference to its worth. For just as the most genuine and most profound love for a human being is not affected by subsequent evidence concerning its causes—indeed, as its triumphant strength is revealed by its survival of the passing of all such causes—so the strength of subjective religiousness is revealed only by the assurance that it has within itself and that gives it a depth and an intensity entirely beyond the causes to which investigation might trace it.

*Contributions to the Epistemology of Religion* [1902]

Pious souls often subscribe to the indistinct notion that religion directly implies, in and of itself, the existence of God or the objective reality of the truth of salvation. It is by no means necessary to deny the legitimacy of religious affirmations, the inspiration of the founders of religion, the reality of their objects and of their interaction with God, in order to maintain that religion as such is even so a product of human consciousness and nothing more. Given that a relationship exists between God and the individual soul, nonetheless, only the aspect constituted by the latter is accessible to us. Religion is not this relationship considered as a whole, as a unity that contains its elements within itself. Whether it is a question of the contractual relationship of the Old Testament, of the filial relationship of the New Testament, or yet of a mystical fusion between God and man, there is always a phenomenon composed of the two directions of a relationship, a metaphysical event that is readily capable of implying or forming the basis of religion but that is *not* religion itself. One might as well say that lawful behavior as a form of individual action is the same thing as the law, as a mode of objective coordination of the relations among people.

Religion, rather, is only the subjective attitude of human beings. As this attitude, it constitutes one aspect of that sum total of relations, or perhaps only the subjective reflection on the reality of that sum total. It is entirely a human way of experiencing, of believing, of acting. It does not matter much through which term people at various times designate the function that constitutes or expresses our share in the relationship between God and us and that is accessible to us only as a condition or an event in our soul. In order to arrive at a scientific analysis of what is religious, it is necessary to depart from a proposition, obvious and yet obscure to so many minds: that a God created and directs the world and renders justice by means of rewards and punishments, that from God derive redemption and sanctification. None of that constitutes religion, even though it would constitute the content of our beliefs, the grounds for our feelings and for our religious actions. Just as it is necessary for us to distinguish from the thinking process itself the objective world that constitutes its content, so we must separate religious content in its objective existence and validity from religion considered as a subjective human process.

This distinction permits religious experience to be reexamined from a very comprehensive epistemological viewpoint. The great categories of our inner life—being and duty, possibility and necessity, willing and fearing—constitute a sequence that allows the contents of our consciousness, the meaning of things with their logical fixing and conceiving, to permeate. One might compare these categories to the diverse, composite forms that one and the same chemical substance can take or to the multiplicity of musical instruments, each with a different timbre, on which one can play the same melody. Perhaps these are only various accompanying feelings which denote the same material content—sometimes as real, sometimes as unreal, sometimes as the object of a duty, sometimes as the object of a hope—or, more precisely, which *mean* that content to be now one thing, now another. According to its overall state, the soul may respond to the same mental image with totally different attitudes. Thus very different implications arise, depending on the context in which the soul accepts that image.

It seems to me that religiosity is one of these formal and fundamental categories and thus brings its own tonality to the contents of certain mental images. In other situations, however, these contents would also permit the application of other categories. Take the facts we just mentioned: God and His relationship to the world, revelation, sin, and redemption can be treated from the pure and simple viewpoint of being—that is, as more or less demonstrable metaphysical facts. Then again, these facts can fall into the category of doubt, that peculiar internal state of oscillation which constitutes a new, specific form of conceiving things, placing them halfway between being and nonbeing. Some of these facts can reappear in the category of duty in such a way that they present themselves, so to speak, as prescriptions that must be satisfied for the outer and inner moral order. Likewise, without their contents being modified in the least, they can be endowed with a religious form—a form perhaps totally unified as it appears to us, an undivided tuning of the soul. This mood gives the content a scope and a specific form of being and of meaning that we can, however, describe psychologically only as a plexus of distinct, composite feelings such as the self, renouncing itself and simultaneously reasserting itself, as a reservoir full of humility and of passionate desire; as an intimate fusion with the supreme principle and separation from it; as sensual immediacy and intangible abstraction of our mental image of it.

That all these terms seem contradictory only makes probable a hypothesis according to which the religious phenomenon is not a composite of these terms, each taken in isolation. Rather, it constitutes an inner unity *sui generis,* whose subsequent construction can be produced only by pairs of contrary psychological terms that limit each other. The same object can circulate through a whole series of domains of interest, each of which assigns to it a particular importance and a specific reaction of our center of volition (intention). Likewise, these transcendental concepts are sometimes based on an inner tension that constitutes their theoretical significance as being or nonbeing. Or they are imbued with a mood that we could call poetic because it is totally beyond reality and that is meant only to benefit from the aesthetic harmony thus attained from the worldview. Or these domains are filled with a specifically religious state of the soul, which perhaps presupposes the transcendent concept and perhaps also justifies it but in any case is not congruent with it. It represents rather well a characteristic key, impossible to confuse with any other, in which our soul plays the melody of those contents.

The theory of religion derives the following benefits from treating the question in this way. *First,* religiosity comes to be viewed as a unified and fundamental state of the soul, so that the significance and reality status that it communicates to its contents are of the same order as the categories of being, duty, willing, and so on. This endows the world it creates with an autonomy that no longer depends on these categories for legitimation; it has the same status as they have. Those categories are related to one another as are *cogitatio* and *extensio* in Spinoza's philosophy: each expresses in its own language everything that exists, and precisely for that reason, neither of the two can invade the other. If religiosity is one of these categories—if it really is, when viewed from a particular perspective, the totality of being—then indeed it is bound to reject not only any testing against the worldviews of reality, of volition, and so on, but also any internal and factual association or connection with them, no matter how much they interfere with each other in the life of the individual. *Second,* the conceptual separation thus achieved between religiosity as such and its more or less dogmatic content has several important consequences. If religiosity is a way of bringing specific conceptual content to mind, one perceives that through all the changes, through all developments of the latter, the depth and the subjective significance of the religious state of the soul can remain the same. Just as all the various contents of being, however alien or contradictory they may appear, share in the same manner and intensity that particular sense of reality which we objectify as their being, likewise all moral prescriptions that enter into conflict partake of the form that gives them a moral character: the form of obligation. From this analysis, then, it also follows that neither does the religious state of the soul logically require any specific content nor does any such content bear within itself the logical necessity to become religion. Neither is it possible to forcibly derive any concrete content from the feeling or category of being; only after it has flowed from other sources can it acquire a certain emotional involvement and thus become a form of being. That content then will show no trace of its indebtedness to emotions. All the old theories that commit the error of seeking to extract God's existence logically from the concept of God, or to deduce the necessity of God from the fact of being, find their counterpart in the dogmatic pretensions that seek always to preserve as legitimate only one kind of content of religiosity. This may be because according to these theories, the religious state of the soul can arrive only at this one kind of content without sinking into internal contradictions. Or it may be that these theories hold that it is possible to enforce logically the specifically religious reaction to the content, which, according to them, follows from their theoretical worldview.

We are delivered from all these difficulties when we conceive of the religious as a fundamental formal category that without doubt requires content as much as does the category of being but that manifests, in the same way as the latter, flexibility in the range of the material content that it can sustain. Finally, this conception delivers religious feeling from every exclusive liaison with transcendent objects. There are an infinite number of affective relationships to some very earthly objects, animate or inanimate, that one can designate only as religious. The response of the person of aesthetic temperament to that which is beautiful to look at; the worker's attitude to his insurgent class; the attitude of the proud feudal lord to his fellow nobles; the response of the soul full of piety to traditions and objects that the past has transmitted to us; the response of the patriot to his country; or the response of the enthusiast to the ideas of liberty, equality, and justice—all these attitudes have in common, in the infinite diversity of their content, a psychological tone that one must designate as religious. Although one can reduce it by analysis to that characteristic interchange of aspiration and enjoyment, of giving and taking, of humility and exaltation, of fusion and separation, one cannot conceive it in its specific unity as composed of these elements.

I am convinced that we will not understand religion in its strict and transcendent sense until we come to interpret it as the result of radicalizing, sublimating, and absolutizing these dispositions, these mixed and undeveloped realizations of its principle. Of course, one does not prejudge in any way by that approach to religion the actual significance of its content, of which it is true to say that it possesses a validity and a plausibility absolutely independent of its historic and psychological origins. Likewise, the attempt to seek the religious form in natural objects to find its beginnings far from religion, properly speaking, does not follow at all in the footsteps of the Greek philosopher Euhemerus. Certainly it is not related to the efforts to dissolve religion into all kinds of human weaknesses. For this is not a question of devaluing religion but, conversely, of raising into its sphere certain worldly relations and feelings. Precisely these phenomena are more rudimentary and less pure realizations of the fundamental principle that appears clearest and most highly developed in religious existence. This method, which saves religion from its incredible isolation without, however, sacrificing even the least of its dignity, becomes possible through the conception of religiosity as a fundamental category, as the same pure form that, like the other fundamental forms existing more or less a priori to our inner being, can accept the entire wealth of reality as its content.

II

Thus the function that endows objects with their religious character is coordinated, theoretically, with that which is essential to their being for us; it is completely independent of genuine psychological development, in which the one entails or presupposes the other and does not occur without it. This accounts more specifically for the distinction between religious belief and theoretical belief. Belief, in the intellectual sense, is of the same order as knowledge; it is merely at a lower level than the latter. It consists in holding something to be true on grounds that are only a little less firm, in a quantitative sense, than those on which we make affirmations of knowledge. In this way investigations of metaphysics or of the theory of knowledge can lead us to hold the existence of God as a plausible and possibly a necessary hypothesis. We then believe in Him as we do in the existence of the diffusion of light through the ether and in the atomic structure of matter. Yet we sense immediately when the religious person says, "I believe in God," that something more is meant than a certain act of holding God's existence to be true.

The best-known theory to be based on this emotion is Kant's theory of practical belief. One of the characteristic themes of eighteenth-century thought was that it is not morality that must be founded on religion; on the contrary, religious belief is the expression of or the consequence of moral conviction. According to Kant,[1] however, belief still remains, by definition, something intellectual, although the point of departure is supratheoretical. That which impels Kant to believe in God and in immortality is the moral necessity of working toward the realization of the "sovereign good," of the harmony of never-perfected virtue and perfect bliss. Because this is an absolute necessity that we cannot give up under any condition insofar as we are moral, we also must believe in the possibility of realizing it, because without this belief all our effort would be devoid of sense. That realization, however, is possible only in transcendent conditions. This supposition obviously does not imply any theoretical proof or knowledge about it. Nevertheless, this Kantian

[1] The French version adds: "comme aussi chez Fichte" (as also with Fichte), Simmel 1903a, 328.

belief remains theoretical. It rests on a twofold conclusion. First, it implies that the imperative that corresponds to the sovereign good cannot exist without leading to the assumption of its realization; second, this realization can occur only through a God and a transcendent justice.

These two claims may be contested. Whether the individual conceives of his moral obligations as part of an objective and absolute development of the sovereign good is a matter of subjective psychological need but not of logical necessity. One can deny or affirm with the same logical justification that morality demands overfulfillment of the duties assigned to each individual. But even granting that such a demand exists, it is far from certain that only transcendent forces can satisfy it. If one were to free this manner of thinking from its strict individualism and to view the action of the individual as a nonautonomous element in the development of humanity, perhaps one could conceive of social adaptation as sufficient for reconciling virtue with bliss in the context of the totality of social fates. Otherwise, in giving the two terms a biological sense, one could allow a purely natural evolution to reach the same destination.

I do not mean to say that these possibilities have fewer difficulties to overcome than the Kantian hypothesis. I introduce them only to demonstrate the possibility of replacing the latter with all sorts of theoretical proposals and in this way shedding light on *its theoretical nature.* Because Kantian belief is nothing immediate but is only the theoretical continuation of moral impulses, nothing would remain of it—absolutely nothing—if the theoretical falsity, or at least the nonnecessity, of the principles that govern this continuation were demonstrated. Therefore Kant, in very meritorious fashion, has established quite well that religious belief exists outside the purely intellectual order, insofar as he states very clearly that faith is not merely a hypothesis that always can be developed into knowledge as such. Religious belief, because its origin and purpose are to be found in morality and not in intellectuality, is completely withdrawn from the intellectual demands of truth. Still, the specific essence of religious belief remains unappreciated because a theoretical character is denied only to occasions that arouse it and to relationships that it sustains, but not to itself. We will therefore still be unable to ascertain its real coloring even if we cease pointing to the dynamics of willing and instead start examining feelings as the source of its being. Anguish, doubt, isolation, and even an overflowing sense of life that passes the limits of the finite can lead to a belief in God. But belief itself still is not defined in this way, because even here it still could be a purely theoretical supposition, even though the same supposition born of emotional needs would result in emotional satisfactions. The most intimate essence of religious belief, it seems to me, can be expressed in this way only: it designates a state of the human soul, an *actuality* and not a simple reflection of an actuality, like all that is theoretical. Intellectuality itself doubtless also designates a certain mode of existence for the soul. But in relation to the role that it plays in the whole of our existence, the mental process itself and the existential form that is expressed by it are effaced entirely in the presence of its content.

As theoretical beings we are nothing but recipients, without individuality—indifferent mirrors of the positive content of things—whose real being disappears totally into the being of the reflected objects. With regard to theoretical knowledge, interest is manifested not in the activity that supports it, but in the factual content of the matter that it supports. By contrast, as long as we have religious beliefs, we do not distinguish ourselves from those who do not have beliefs or who have different beliefs by the diversity of content that mirrors our consciousness—this diversity does not hold any particular importance for the notion considered here—but by the state of our soul itself. Moreover, religious belief in God is a form of inner being that can have its theoretical side as well as its theoretical consequences and can be expressed well in theoretical form, whereas in theoretical belief or knowledge about God our psychic state is only the impersonal and hidden support of the content of a mental image.

This is true not only of belief in God's existence, but also of what a religious soul calls knowledge of God in the broader sense. This is not becoming conscious of God as the content of a mental image but rather as an emotional fusion with Him experienced as a *real event*. This experience comprises the act of giving ourselves to God and the act of receiving God. The attempt to form a mental image of God is only a looking-glass reflection of these events. It is the foundation of the statement by Gregory of Nyssa: "The person who has emptied his heart of all wickedness sees in his own beauty the reflection of the divine essence." Any theoretical belief can change its content without the individual's becoming someone else in the process, because the *function* of believing remains unchanged. But in religious belief this mutual independence of content and function does not exist: belief in a different god is a different believing. The same applies to emotional ties among humans; if love turns away from one person and toward another, it not only changes its object but also, the deeper it is, the more it reaches down to our very existence, the more it is a different love. Whether one believes in Jehovah, the Christian God, in Ormuzd and Ahriman, in Vitzliputzli—that makes a difference not only in content but also in function; it proclaims a different human *existence*.

Thanks to this interpretation—according to which religious belief is a form of existence, is a subjective process itself, and is not, as in theoretical knowledge, its content—all kinds of facts are explained that would otherwise be paradoxical. For example, there is prayer to obtain faith—completely senseless behavior from the standpoint of common rationality because one evidently can address the prayer only to one in whom one already believes. And because one already believes, one no longer needs to pray to obtain belief. In reality, this prayer presupposes belief in the theoretical sense. To be able to pray, one must dismiss both doubt that God exists and doubt that God is in a position to answer prayers. But that one acts in this way proves that one prays to obtain something else, an actual inner reality, a transformation of the way we are that finds in the holding of something to be true only a point of conscious support or an external reflection. Such, perhaps, is the profound basis of the ontological error that seeks to arrive at the existence of God through reasoning by pure thought. This reasoning is possible only if the existence of God already has been tacitly presupposed. One has placed Him in a perfectly good conscience among the premises, so to speak, because one feels that we already possess God, that logic will merely demonstrate this, because religious belief in God is part of our actual existence, from which belief or theoretical proof originates as a secondary reflex. This is the reverse of the case of prayer to obtain belief, but it rests on the same basis: in prayer to obtain belief, given the theoretical significance of belief, one would like to arrive at its significance for being. In reasoning, given the sure feeling of being, one would like to obtain or formulate from it theoretical legitimation.

This idea can perhaps also be worded as follows: the unity of the religious condition unfolds in two directions. In the intellectual direction, it results in theoretical mental images of the existence of the facts of salvation; in the direction of the mind, it results in emotion. If we now conduct circular argumentation to (theoretically) believe in God because we feel Him, although we really cannot feel Him until we have accepted His existence, this is perfectly legitimate; it is an expression of that union. If a unified impulse A breaks down into its components $\alpha$ and $\beta$, it happens very frequently that $\alpha$ can only be proved through $\beta$ and $\beta$ in turn through $\alpha$. Thus it appears to be a circular argument that we sacrifice for an object because it is valuable and that it is valuable because we cannot obtain it without sacrifice. This circle represents the unity of our fundamental attitude about the value of the object.[2] The Kantian critique is correctly directed against the ontological proof as an intellectual construct. In addition, however, I consider it important to note how such a grossly false conclusion could have been reached. This occurred because an emotion or a subjective state of mind was transposed into a merely theoretical concept, which then lacked any fecundity.

On this basis, the multiple moral value judgments that one sees attached to belief are indeed explained. That belief could be something of merit would be totally absurd, in the purely intellectual sense of the word. That one allows oneself to be convinced of something theoretically is completely beyond the qualities of morality and immorality. The total moral perversity that can coexist with a belief in the existence of God, exempt from doubt, should suffice to prove the absence of a link between the two orders of facts. Therefore the belief that is held to be meritorious must be something else, signifying only an immediate and inner personal quality. Conversely, it is the same when the Church makes incredulity into a moral offense. The disastrous influence created by this opinion, moreover, need not be analyzed. It consists principally of the following: that the quality of inner being that makes up belief has been carelessly confounded with morals. Furthermore, granting the moral sense of belief, we have neglected the idea that the total corresponding constitution of the soul also could have been produced by other qualities and movements inside it. Finally, faith, as having this significance, has been identified carelessly with one kind of content of belief to the exclusion of all others.

It is doubtless objectionable to interpret faith as a practical maxim. But this maxim was based, after all, on an instinct that was something more and deeper than hierarchical intolerance:

[2] I have followed up this theoretical axiom of valuation in my book *Philosophie des Geldes* (Philosophy of money) ([1900] 1978) [footnote by Simmel].

the very fundamental feeling that faith is not merely a theoretical assumption that would pass over our existence as indifferently as the assumption that Sirius is inhabited. Rather this feeling implied that faith itself is a form of being. It not only is a theoretical statement with profound *consequences* for our essence — for those could have been attributed to us just as little as their causes — but is determined by our essence, or rather is itself a determinant of that essence.

**PART 5** *Toward a "Broader" Perspective on Religion*

**ELEVEN** *Religion [1912 (1906)]*

## 1. RELIGION AND THE GREAT FORMS OF EXISTENCE

It is not uncommon for personal or material forces to enter our lives in a somewhat disruptive manner; we may regard them as intrusive or inappropriate, but when they present themselves with enhanced urgency, significantly increasing the demands they impose on us, they lose this intrusive character. That which could not be made compatible as a subordinate element with other elements of the life with which it has become interwoven can establish an organic, fulfilled relationship to these other elements if it is allowed to become life's absolute and dominating force. An amorous affection, an ambition, or a newly acquired interest often will fail to fit comfortably with the existing constellation of an individual's life; but as soon as passion or resolve places it at the center of the soul and gears the whole of existence toward it, life's very basis is completely renewed and can gain a whole new sense of harmony and integration. [This form of fate has frequently become real in connection with religious developments within the individual. Whenever the ideals and demands of religion come into conflict not only with basic instincts but also with intellectual and moral norms and values, the way out of such confusion and uncertainty has been found only when the religious ideals cease to be relative and acquire complete dominance. Not until religion sets the fundamental tone for life can life's single elements once more interrelate harmoniously with each other and with the whole.

Of course, one element can assert itself as the dominating

*Note:* This is the revised and augmented second edition of 1912. The first edition appeared in 1906. Arabic numerals indicate original chapters by Simmel. The titles have been inserted by the editor. Brackets [ ] enclose passages that were inserted or revised in the 1912 edition.

factor in this way only after a severe struggle with other elements, which are bound to lose out in this new configuration. If we accept that a *majority* of such demands are justified—according to their own inner requirements as well as according to their potential to organize and unify life—we are initially faced with a conflict that, if life is not to remain hopelessly divided in its fundamental potential, must be resolvable at least in principle, at least in theory. Theoretical speculation provides us with a possible solution to this conflict.]

When the problem of the coexistence of physical and mental being began to worry philosophers, Spinoza resolved the irreconcilability by stating that extension, on the one hand, and thought, on the other, each expressed the whole of existence in its own language. The two thus were able to coexist as soon as each was no longer relative to the other but could claim the totality of the world for itself and could represent this totality in its own way. [The most general of maxims thus would state that *each* of the great forms of our existence must be proved capable of expressing the whole of life in its own terms.][1] The organization of our existence through the absolute domination of a single principle at the expense of all the others would then be raised to a higher plane: none would have any cause to feel threatened by any other within its own independently formed view of the world, because it would accept the others' right to form the world in their own way. Theoretically, these different interpretations of the world then would be no more likely to hinder each other than would musical sounds be likely to clash with colors. [The basis for this idea is the distinction between the forms of existence, on the one hand, and its content, on the other. In its most primitive application, it is the principle by which we mold the same material in a multitude of different ways, or mold countless materials into the same shape. Such

---

[1] Insertion replaces a similar statement in the 1906 edition.

a principle is the most comprehensive scheme for the construction of a world and for interpreting all lifestyles. All the various ways in which man lives by his actions, knowledge, feelings, and creativity might be regarded as types or categories that are imposed on existence. Though the raw material of this existence may be infinitely varied, it remains the same within each of the categories, and each of the categories has the fundamental capacity to shape the totality of this raw material according to its own laws.

The artist as well as the scientist, the epicurean as well as the pragmatist, all are faced with the sensory impressions, impulses, and destinies that confront them in the world and provide the same raw material for existence. Every person—insofar as he is purely an artist or a thinker, a bon vivant or a man of action—will create from this material a particular kind of universe for himself. Of course we must take into account the fact that what one person has created can provide the raw material for another, and that every such form of existence, as it manifests itself at a historical point in the infinite development of our species, can acquire this material only in fragmentary form and in constantly changing conditions. We also must bear in mind that we can probably never grasp this material in pure form because it will always present itself as a preformed component of some world. We may interpret the multiplicity and the unity of these mentally formed worlds thus: they are form-giving categories, each of which represents a complete, self-contained world, entirely uniform in inspiration and motivation. All of these worlds are constructed from the same material, the basic components of the world, which become artistic, practical, or theoretical depending on the synthesis imposed on them by the mind but also are held together by the uniform course of spiritual life.] For the latter always picks out only fragments from the multiplicity of these worlds—which present themselves to us or within us as potential ideas, so to speak—to form a life from them, although the soul's instability of purpose and temperament often causes these various fragments to conflict sharply with one another.

To the naive person, the world of experience and practice simply is reality, and the contents of this world exist as something perceivable and manipulable. If such contents are formed within the categories of art or religion, of the emotions or of philosophical reflection, then this formative process either is regarded as a superstructure imposed on "real" existence or else is separate from reality but becomes interwoven with it to shape the rich diversity of life—just as alien or even hostile fragments intrude in the course of an individual's life but become part of the integrated whole. This standpoint can lead to uncertainties and confusion in the various views of the world and of life, but such difficulties disappear immediately if we recognize that so-called reality itself is yet another of those forms which shape the existing contents of life—the very same contents that we can arrange in an artistic, religious, or scientific way or in the manner of a game. Reality certainly is not *the* world per se but is only *one* world alongside the worlds of art or religion, the same material cast in a different mold and proceeding from different assumptions. The empirically "real" world is probably that order of existing elements which best serves the survival and development of the life of our species.

As acting beings, we register reactions from the world around us, and the usefulness or harmfulness of these reactions depends on the ideas that inform our actions. We describe as reality that world of ideas or way of visualizing things which will enable us to act in a manner that is appropriate to the psychobiological organization peculiar to our species. For beings of a different nature and with differing needs, there would be another "reality," because different action would be beneficial to their living conditions. That is, their actions would be based on a different view of the world. Thus purposes and fundamental assumptions decide which "world" is created by the psyche, and the real world is only one of many possible worlds. Yet within ourselves there are basic needs other than those of a general, practical nature, and these also create worlds. Art, too, draws on the elemental contents of reality, but what turns these into art is that they are given forms that are based on the artistic need for visual or emotional appeal or for particular emphasis and that transcend reality. For example, even the spatial structure within a painting is different from that of reality. The clear sense of harmony and emotional expression in art could never be found in reality. One might speak of a particular logic, a certain concept of truth, and certain laws with which art creates a new world alongside reality itself, formed from the very same raw material as the latter and representing an equivalent to it.

The same might be said to apply to religion. From the same concrete and conceptual material as we experience in the context of reality, the world of religion emerges, with new tensions, new dimensions, and new syntheses. The concepts of soul and existence, of destiny and guilt, of fortune and sacrifice, right down to the hair on one's head and the sparrow on the rooftop—all of these form the content of the *religious* world as well. There, however, they are colored by values and emotional emphases that assign them to different dimensions, as it were, and subject them to adjustments in perspective, just as when the very same material is molded by philosophy, art, or the empirical order. Religious life creates the world anew; it represents the whole of existence in a particular key, so that in its pure form it *cannot* come into conflict with those world constructs created according to the other categories—even though an individual's life may pass through all these various levels and cause them to become confused and discordant, because he cannot grasp them in their fullness but can only grasp fragments of each.

This was the thrust of the reflections at the beginning of this essay: if an element of life that cannot coexist passively with other elements is raised to the status of an absolute and ultimate principle of life, it becomes fully reconcilable with all other elements. Only when one realizes that religion provides the totality of a complete worldview, along with other theoretical or practical totalities, does it become a fully coherent system free of internal turbulence, just as all these other systems do also. [This idea or claim is not influenced by its purity being only rarely respected by life itself. Just as we spoke above of an artistic logic, it is also possible to speak of a religious logic that can recognize evidence, form concepts, and convey values appropriately—albeit in a way that no other system of logic would ever permit. But like the logic of science, religious logic claims often enough to encompass or to govern all others within itself. Whenever this has happened, religion has acquired idolatrous, statutory, and profane elements, that is, such elements as are subject to a different and nonreligious system of logic. Here we see the most universal, almost inevitable difficulties associated with religion: it derives from needs and impulses of the soul that do not have the least to do with the "things" of the empirical world and with rational criteria. Instead of constructing their own autonomous life world, these impulses become realized as claims rooted in a seemingly self-evident context that imposes itself unquestioningly. It is inevitable that such claims concerning this world and the hereafter come into conflict with intellectual standards that have an entirely different origin.

The need to find completeness in the fragmentary nature of man's existence, to reconcile conflicts within the individual and between men, the need for a fixed point in all the instability that surrounds us, for a just purpose in and behind the cruelties of life, for unity in and above life's bewildering multiplicity, and for an absolute object toward which to direct our humility and our desire for contentment—all of this nourishes man's ideas about the transcendent sphere: man's hunger feeds these ideas. The person of absolutely pure faith does not care whether these ideas are theoretically possible or impossible; he simply feels inwardly that his yearning has found an outlet and a sense of fulfillment in his faith. The question of whether the religious dogmas that develop in this way are "true" in the sense of an empirical experience or a scientific statement might be said to be of only secondary importance. The crucial point is that such dogmas are believed and are felt to be true, and their truth is only the indirect or complementary expression of the intense, inward yearning that has led to them—rather as some powerful subjective sensation might compel us to believe in the existence of an object equivalent to it, even though logic would cause us to doubt the existence of such an object. Even if the unity of the religious world, emanating from its very center and providing its most profound justification, were to remain a mere aspiration, whose fulfillment in any pure sense the composite nature of empirical man hinders, it nonetheless demonstrates why religion never can be identical with ethics, as is claimed, for the latter is itself a category that is capable of forming a world of its own.

One need not even dwell on the differences between the world of ethics and that of religion; that they are both *worlds* means that each imposes its own order on all the contents of the world according to its own ultimate principles. But if one were introduced completely or partially into the other, that would be enough to create the same contradiction that Spinoza saw in the blending of the physical and the mental world. There can be no doubt that man, as I suggested above, with the limited powers and interests at his disposal, only ever realizes small fragments of these possible worlds, which actually exist only in an ideal, conceptual form. Just as he does not mold all directly given content into scientific knowledge or artistic creation, so everything in the world does not become part of religion as a whole, because this molding process does not encounter equally malleable material in all the components of world and mind, though such a process is essentially possible everywhere.

Whether the material shaped by religion is raw or preformed, whether it is pure or impure, religion in the historical sense can develop only on the basis of such worldly content. Religiousness in its pure essence, free of all empirical material, is a *life;* the religious person is somebody who *lives* in a certain way peculiar to himself, and whose spiritual processes display a rhythm, a key, an arrangement, and a proportion of spiritual energies that are unmistakably distinct from those of a theoretical, artistic, or practical person. Yet all of this is a question of process, not of a concrete formation: this life, this operation must encompass actual *contents* if describable and "objective" religions are to come into existence. This occurs in the same way in which the a priori categories of knowledge form the theoretical world. And just as these categories of reason facilitate knowledge without being knowledge themselves, so the religious forms of sin and redemption, love and faith, dedication and self-assertion make religion possible as impulses within life. Yet they *are* not in themselves religion, just as the material that life raises to religious status is not religious in itself. Pursuing a characteristic path not identical to historical progression but reflecting the latter's typically recurring patterns of meaning, these two factors of form and content become merged as follows: the religious mood of man, a characteristic evolving pattern of his life process, causes all possible spheres in which this process takes place to be experienced as religious spheres; then, from this general religious mood of life, the process of religion acquires a physical, objective form.

The religious current penetrates the contents of life, which otherwise are molded according to intellectual, practical, or artistic principles, and draws them up into the transcendent sphere in their new form. Thus religiosity as an inner quality of life or a unique kind of existence acquires its substance only when it pervades the material diversity of the world, thereby coming face to face with itself, as it were: the world of religion on the one hand and the religious subject on the other. It must first tinge the elements of the world with its own particular quality of experience to be able to surpass the other forms into which such elements might be shaped, and to proceed to construct from this fully fledged religiousness the numerous worlds of faith with their gods and doctrines. One might thus enumerate three domains of life that exemplify this transposition into the religious key: the behavior of man toward the external, natural world, his behavior toward fate, and his behavior toward the human world around him. If such behavior is religious in its primary essence, we might say that it "creates" the finished product of religion as a form within which the religious quality has acquired concrete shape and content. It is our task here to develop this interpretation in relation to the last-mentioned category of behavior. In doing so, we shall first make reference to the other two categories, creating a framework that will help to illustrate the fundamental view of religiousness on which this essay is based.]

It is a well-worn cliché that religion is no more than an exaggeration of empirical-psychical facts that are determined by our natural state. Thus God as creator of the world may appear as a hypertrophy of our inclination to seek underlying causes; the religious sacrifice can be viewed as a perpetuation of the necessity, with which we are familiar from practical experience, that everything we desire has its price; and the fear of God may present itself as the heightening and magnified reflection of the supreme power of physical nature itself, to which we are constantly exposed. [This hypothesis, however, is utterly superficial. If these religious motifs were merely augmentations or solidifications of physical phenomena, the empirical-sensory conditions themselves would not account for such motifs, so this reductionist view in fact conceals the real issue here.] Surely religious categories must be the basic point of departure and must effectively shape the material from the outside if it is to acquire religious significance and to be molded into religious phenomena. [It is not empirical contents that are exaggerated to form religious phenomena: instead, the religious components within the empirical world are given special emphasis.] The objects of experience become *knowable* because the categories and criteria of knowledge have formed them from their raw state as sensory impressions; we derive the law of causality from our experiences because we shape our experiences according to this law. Indeed, it is this law that allows them to become "experiences" in the first place.

In the very same way, things gain religious significance and are raised to a transcendent level because and insofar as they have been subsumed under the religious category from the outset; this category has determined their constitution, even before they are fully recognized as religious phenomena. If God as creator really derives from the compulsion to extend the chain of causes, then the religious constituent that aims at the transcendent is present at the very beginning in the chain of causes. Of course, this chain remains firmly within the domain of concrete knowledge and logically joins each link in the chain with the next, but the restless rhythm of the causal process has a certain quality of uneasy dissatisfaction with all that exists, apparently degrading each single link to overwhelming insignificance in relation to the vast chain as a whole. In short, the causal scheme itself has religious undertones. The same line of thought leads us either to a world accessible to empirical knowledge or to a point of transcendence, depending on the level on which we pursue it and the emotional emphasis with which we invest it. God as cause of the world is the crystallized inner meaning of a process rooted in the religious category, whereas the abstract law of causality is the formula extracted from the process of causality as pursued in the category of knowledge. The infinite extension of the chain of causes as applied to the empirical world would never logically conclude the existence of a God, and the perceivable world of itself would never have made the leap into the world of religion —were it not that this causal scheme could also be pursued under the aegis of religious sensibility, for which God as creator is the ultimate expression, the substance by which religiosity can take root as a living impulse and meaning within this causal process.

It is easier to comprehend how our *emotional* ties with physical nature can develop in a religious context, and how in such a development religion takes on a concrete, objective form, separate from its subjective form. Our natural surroundings can stimulate aesthetic pleasure within us, but also terror and fear, a sense of awe at their supreme power—the former when we suddenly perceive as accessible and comprehensible that which we ordinarily feel to be alien and eternally distinct from us, the latter when something purely physical, and as such entirely transparent and indifferent, acquires a terrifyingly impenetrable obscurity. Nature also can stimulate within us a fundamental response that is difficult to analyze, and that I can describe only as a feeling of being profoundly shaken: when we are moved deeply, not by the extraordinary beauty or grandeur of a natural phenomenon but often by a ray of sunlight gleaming through the leaves or by the swaying of a branch in the wind—something that does not appear to be of any special significance but that reveals a hidden consonance with the foundations of our being and thus allows us to sense the passionate emotions of our inner being. All these sensations can occur without extending beyond their immediate domain—that is, without acquiring any religious significance. They also can acquire such significance, however, without any change in their content. Such impulses sometimes stimulate within us a certain tension or impetus, a sense of humility or gratitude, as if a soul were speaking to us through these impulses. All of this can only be described as religious, but it does not constitute religion itself: it is the process by which religion emerges, by extending itself into the transcendent sphere, materializing its essence as its object and apparently receiving itself once more in return.

The idea that the beauty, formation, and order of the world indicate that an absolute power must have constructed it according to purposive principles—what has been called the teleological proof of the existence of God—is no more than the logical configuration of this religious process. Certain types of sensitivity toward nature are thus experienced in the religious category as well as in the purely subjective, aesthetic, or metaphysical categories. Just as an empirical object marks the point at which a number of sensory impressions converge, or the point to which they are extended, the object of religion is also such a point: feelings such as those described converge there by taking on this external, objective form. Because all of these feelings have flowed together to create an object, which thus is a product of all of them, this object appears to the *individual* as the point of all religious emanation, a preexistent state of being. [Religious *life,* actively molding the content of the world, takes on its own religious *substance* in this object. At this point and for all that follows, it should be noted that we are not dealing in any way with the *reality* of religious objects beyond human spiritual consciousness of those objects and their significance in this sense. What we are engaging in here is and remains a purely psychological analysis, because we are tracing not the historical development of religious ideas but what might be called the logic of psychology—that is, the sensory patterns that would help us to understand how the actual historical developments came about.]

The second domain in which the soul can enter the religious category is that of fate. Fate might be defined as the forces affecting the development of the person by that which is not part of himself—whether or not his own actions or being have a role to play in these determining forces. Because this is a point at which the inner and the outer sphere come into contact, the concept of destiny, viewed from the inner perspective, involves an element of randomness. Even if fate manifests itself as the very executor of the subjectively determined meaning of life, the random element still displays its fundamental conflict with this subjective meaning. Whatever our subjective reaction to fate, whether submissive or rebellious, hopeful or despairing, demanding or contented, it can be entirely irreligious or entirely religious. [Because of its externality, all "fate" contains something that is not comprehensible to us, and in this it acquires the religious cachet. This also is the case because whatever happens by chance is still meaningful, provided that it is experienced as providential. If we experience what happens to us by chance under the category of fate, it becomes more bearable in spite of its painful nature because it will appear to be oriented toward us and stripped of its indifference. Chance thus acquires a certain dignity, which is our own: fate has the effect of elevating man's status. That is, what was a series of chance happenings is molded into a certain meaningful pattern related to ourselves, however problematic it may be. In this way the concept of fate has a structure that predisposes it to absorb the religious frame of mind, which takes the notion of fate and solidifies the concept of predestination.] The important point here is that the religious hue does not emanate from a transcendent power that is believed to exist, but is a particular quality of feeling itself, a focus or impetus, a solemnity or sense of remorse that is in itself religious. Thus religion generates its subject matter as its objectification or counterpart, just as empirical sensation creates its object.

Although the contents of fate are by definition independent of us, our experience of fate in the specific domain of religion is molded by the productive religious forces that lie at the heart of our being. Experience thus corresponds to the categories of religious objectiveness because these categories themselves have molded it. "For those who love God, all things are bound to turn out for the best": this saying illustrates not that things are simply there and that the hand of God reaches down from out of the clouds and arranges them to the advantage of His beloved children, but that the religious person's own experience of things is such that they can provide him only with the blessing he strives for as a person of faith. No matter what course a destiny might take within the categories of earthly fortune, outward success, or intellectual comprehensibility, within the category of religion it will always be accompanied by such emotional tensions, arranged according to such a pattern of value, transfigured by such interpretations—all of which are necessarily geared to religious significance and to the idea that God takes care of His children in the best possible way—just as the world must pursue a causally logical course because, at an epistemological level, it is formed by the underlying principle of causality. [To no lesser an extent, the formal breadth that fate possesses in all the categories of life makes it suited to transpose the impulse of religious life from an ideal to an actuality and to the concept of the absolute divinity. A motif from German mysticism may illustrate this point. In Eckhart's view, God is the epitome of simplicity and uniformity, though He encompasses all manifold beings within Him; these constitute God Himself, but at the same time are "as nothing" within Him. He created the world, and yet He did not, since creation is eternal. God "pervades all created beings and yet remains untouched by everything"; He is in things and yet also is "as much" above them. The soul exists through God and is nothing without Him, and yet God too is nothing without the soul. Beholding God is the same as being beheld by God.

All of these and many similar ideas have been described as contradictory and irreconcilable, but the inspirational principle behind them has been missed: any conceivable relationship between God and the world must be real! In mysticism, this is the form adopted by the *ens realissimum,* replacing the objective God with a relationship to God—the one religious fact that offers itself as the most immediate objectification of the subjective life process of religion. Thus the very *breadth* of our destinies, molded by the inward religious function of life, may often point this spiritual function to a sense of the limitless expanse of the divine.] Just as cognition does not create causality, but instead causality creates cognition, so religion does not create religiosity, but religiosity creates religion. The workings of fate, as man experiences it in a certain subjective mood, consist of an interweaving of relationships, meanings, and feelings that do not yet make up religion in themselves and whose factual substance would never be linked with religion by souls in a different mood. Separated from these actualities, however, and [cemented together by the religiosity that pervades them, so to speak,] these elements constitute an objective realm of their own, and thus form "religion"—that is, the world of the objects of faith.

I come at last to the relationships of human beings to the human world and to the currents of religion that flow within them; within these relationships, too, energies and sources of meaning take effect, on which religious significance has not been imposed externally from some already existing source. [Rather they carry it within them as a disposition of the individuals in question, so that, conversely, religion develops from them as a mental-objective pattern.] Religion in its fully developed state, the entire spiritual complex associated with the transcendent sphere, presents itself as the absolute and unified form of the feelings and impulses that social life itself develops in a tentative and apparently experimental fashion[, insofar as it is religiously oriented as a mood or function]. In order to understand this, it is necessary to consider the principle of sociological structure just as we have already considered that of religious structure. The life of society consists of interactions between its elements — interactions which in part are no more than momentary actions and reactions, and which in part acquire concrete form in offices and laws, structures and possessions, language and other means of communication. All of these social relationships come about as a result of certain interests, purposes, and urges, which make up what one might call the fabric of society: the existence of individuals in social groups, with all of their indifference and affection, mutual support and conflict. This material of life can remain constant while assuming a multitude of such forms in alternation. Conversely, the unchanging forms of interaction can apply themselves to the most diverse material. Thus the norms and products of public life can be borne equally by the free interplay of competing forces and by the regulatory control of lower elements by higher ones. A great many social interests may be preserved in any given period by family organization, for example, whereas the same interests are passed on later or elsewhere to professional associations or state bureaucracies.

One of the most characteristic forms of social life, one of those fixed norms of life by which society ensures that its mem-

bers behave in an appropriate and beneficial way, is that of custom—in less sophisticated cultures the only generally characteristic form of socially determined behavior. The very same living
conditions of society that are later codified and enforced by the
power of state, on the one hand, or are left to the discretion of
the cultured and well-bred individual, on the other—these conditions are guaranteed in small, primitive social groups through
that remarkable and direct supervision of the individual by his
environment which is called custom. Custom, law, and individual morality are varying combinations of social elements, all
of which can be based on the very same principles of behavior
and which in fact occur in diverse forms among various peoples
at different times in history. Among the social forms that allow
the community to encourage the individual to act appropriately
are the religions. The religious character of social conditions has
very often been one characteristic stage of their development.
In a given period, an aspect of social life that previously and
subsequently is represented by different forms of relationship
between human beings will adopt a religious form. This is most
obvious in the case of legislation, which at certain times and in
certain places is theocratic and is determined fully by religious
sanction, whereas elsewhere it is guaranteed by state authority
or by custom. Indeed, it seems that the indispensable requirements of society took the form of an integrated, undifferentiated whole in which there was no distinction between moral,
religious, and judicial sanctions—for example, the *dharma* of the
Indians, the *themis* of the Greeks, and the *fas* of the Romans—
and that, according to the various historical circumstances, one
form or another finally became the agent of such social order.

[Here and there it is possible to discover more about the
historical stages of this development. For example, it is re-
ported that before and during the Roman period, the Egyptians
were willing to endure foreign occupation—perhaps did not
even notice it—if only their religious ideas and customs were
not interfered with, because these almost solely constituted the

whole life form of the country. This shows how the fundamental principle of social norms applied; for the purposes of practical consciousness, this principle was represented by or focused mainly on only one of the elements latent within it, namely religion. The all-encompassing, absolute dominance of Egyptian religious life, but also its vague and mysterious character, can perhaps be explained if we regard the religious factor as having outwardly become a distinct aspect of this previously undifferentiated concept of socially acceptable norms. Inwardly, however, such norms still were identified entirely with religion.] This often retrograde cultural development of social norms—from custom to law and vice versa, from obligatory humanitarianism to religious sanction and vice versa—is in some way connected with another characteristic of social development: some practical and theoretical elements of life evolve in the course of history from full consciousness to tacit and subconscious acceptance and practice, while other elements—sometimes the very same ones—develop conversely from the subconscious, instinctive stage to that of conscious formulation and accountability. Much more conscious control is exerted over our actions if they are determined by law than if they are governed by custom; free morality, defined by the individual conscience, attributes to the impulses of our actions the state of consciousness or unconsciousness quite differently than does social regulation.

In the case of a religious sanction, much greater tension exists between obscure concurrent feelings and the clear sense of its purpose than in the case of a sanction imposed by custom, and so forth. A characteristic feature of such development is that the change in intensity of a social relationship leads to an increase in the sanctions imposed on it. In periods of intense patriotism, for example, the relationship of the individual to his group acquires a certain fervor and dedication that not only are of a religious character but are an act of religiosity; there is also at such times a far more pressing need to invoke divine authority; the individual's impulses become much more directly part of religious excitement than during uneventful periods, when such relationships are defined by convention or by laws of the state. At the same time, however, this fervor represents an increased *awareness*[2] of patriotic relationships. Such situations that are characterized by danger and passionate agitation, where the triumph of a political entity is at stake, lend the individual's subjective response to the situation a religious quality and structure. In such a case his awareness of his own relationship to the group will be much stronger than during periods when the other norms apply, from which this more intense subjective involvement derives and to which it ultimately returns.

Private relationships that are open to religious certification also frequently attract it at times when the individual's awareness is most focused on them: with marriage, for example, at the point when matrimony is actually entered into; or, during the Middle Ages, when contracts of different types were entered into. The Puritans' life was characterized by a chronic obsession with consciously recording every moment of life, an active account of every thought and deed, because the religious norm reigned despotically over all details of life and did not recognize any other form of sanction. Yet the reverse is also true: the crucial importance of the mainly prehistoric social form of tribal organization decreases with the growth of state power to a merely religious phenomenon. Of course, tribal systems were always cult groups as well, but in addition they represented a shared place of residence, property, justice, and weapons. They obviously must have been much more at the center of individual awareness than in those epochs in which membership in a tribe or a kinship group meant no more than joining in festivals and sacrifices with other members, as in late antiquity or in contemporary China. In these cases, the exclusively religious nature of group sanctions accompanied a diminished sense of group unity

[2]Emphasized only in the 1912 edition, not in that of 1906.

and a decrease in its importance. [The converse development applies to the sacred and criminal law of the Romans. The Romans' straightforward, down-to-earth logic apparently rejected the *bis in idem,* whereby the same offense incurred both earthly and divine punishment. If the criminal judge took the matter in hand, the priest had to withdraw his authority, because the idea that everything on earth was subject to yet another higher authority was quite alien to this particular nation. This allows us to note that in the case of this particular people the moral importance of religion recedes as offenses originally penalized by ecclesiastical law fall within the domain of criminal law.]

We have by no means exhausted the possible types of social norms, but at least we have made a plausible case that all these types of norm are merely varying general psychic categories and their transformation merely formal alterations to the same practical content of life. Of course, when the norm-defining agency is religion, the religion already must be in existence; the key point here, however, is not the dogmatic ideas about transcendent beings, which represent only the means of sanction, but the acquisition of a sense of solemnity and stability for what is socially required, expressing its full social significance in a particular key and with a force not otherwise possible. Thus the social norm reaches a new stage in its development.

Sanitary codes were imposed as divine commandments, as in the case of ancient Jewish legislation. In Teutonic Christendom in the seventh and eighth centuries, murder and perjury passed under ecclesiastical jurisdiction and were treated by the bishop as offenses against the divine order, punishable by penance. Princes and sovereigns claimed obedience from their subjects on the basis of divine right. None of these social conditions would ever have risen to religious significance if they had not first had social importance. [Neither would this religious significance have developed if the life process of which these conditions formed a part were not essentially religious in character, even before it expressed itself in a social or any other form.

Certain sociological relations, however, have a significance and an emotive component that predestine them to assume a religious form. The religious phenomenon, or some of its features, can develop in a social setting; later they gain a distinct, purely religious significance because the social context forms a kind of channel through which this particular mood can flow. The mood maintains its basic course, and yet from the social context it develops a form or a substance, a potential concretization. The social conditions] themselves would not attract this transcendent significance—just as many other social norms often associated with such conditions have not done so—if *their* particular emotional content, *their* unifying power, and *their* limited scope did not predispose them to projection onto the religious plane.

## 2. RELIGION AND SOCIAL RELATIONSHIPS

The underlying basis on which the religious category [permeates and molds social relationships, which in turn have the potential to make the religious tangible] is provided by the remarkable analogy between the individual's behavior toward the deity and his behavior towards society. An especially important aspect is his sense of dependence. The individual feels bound to some general, higher principle from which he originates and to which he ultimately returns, to which he dedicates himself but from which he also expects elevation and redemption, from which he is distinct and to which he is yet identical. God has been called the *coincidentia oppositorum,* the unifying point in which all the irreconcilable, conflicting forces of existence are fused into one. Included in this concept is the extraordinary diversity of attitudes of the soul toward God and of God toward the human soul. Love and alienation, humility and pleasure, delight and regret, despair and trust—these are not simply the passing changes in the soul's feelings toward its God: each leaves a lasting impression on the soul's fundamental relationship to its God, so that the soul appears to hold all these conflicting currents within itself and simultaneously to emanate them. And the God Himself is just, but He also forgives in a way that goes beyond justice. In the ancient world, and not only there, he stands above factions; yet he takes sides. He is the absolute master of the world and yet allows it to develop according to its own inevitable laws.

The interaction between the human being and his God thus encompasses the whole range of possible relationships, both sequentially and simultaneously. In doing so it unmistakably reiterates the behavioral patterns that exist between the individual and his social group. Here we see the same phenomenon of an individual subjected to a supreme power yet permitted a degree of freedom; passive reception that still allows room for a responsive reaction; the self-surrender that does not exclude rebellion; the mixture of reward and punishment; the relationship of a single member to the whole, even though that single member still desires to be a whole himself. One feature of religion in particular can be transposed to the relationship of the individual to the group: that is the humility with which the pious person attributes everything he is and has to God's generosity and sees in divine power the source of his being and strength. For man is not absolutely nothing in relation to God: though only a grain of dust, he is not an utterly insignificant force but is at least a receptacle ready to receive its contents. Thus there are strong similarities between the religious and the sociological forms of existence. The latter need only be accompanied or received by an inner sense of religion to produce concrete religion as a separate form of existence and behavior. Without having this general idea in mind—and thus providing better evidence of its accuracy—a specialist gives the following account of the ancient Semitic religion: "In the period immediately preceding Islam, there was a marked lack of religion in the usual sense of the word among the Arab heroes; they were very little concerned with gods and godly things and were extremely negligent in matters of worship. Yet they regarded the tribe with a certain religious awe, and the life of a fellow member was sacred and inviolable to them. One can comprehend this apparent contradiction in light of the ancient world, for which the god and his people formed a community within which the relationships of the faithful among themselves found the same expression as their relationship toward their deity. The original religious community was the tribe, and all of the obligations that derived from kinship were simultaneously components of religious life. Even if the tribal god receded into insignificance and eventually fell into almost total obscurity, the essence of the tribal religion continued to assert itself in the lasting sacredness of the blood bond."

[Thus there exist social conditions or interpersonal relationships that might be described as semireligious in form. These types of relationship, having become detached from their social context and raised to the transcendental dimension, constitute religion in its narrower sense as a self-contained sphere. While the surface of these phenomena produces various disguises and skews, their relationships can clearly be noticed. There is, for example, the religious—or, if the ugly term be permitted, religioid—factor, which anybody of deep sensitivity will find in any surrender or acceptance. As a purely sociological phenomenon, this has nothing to do with the specific sphere of religion. Yet its inherent structure bears an almost indefinable spiritual resemblance to an aspect of religiousness in general that becomes crystallized in the fully developed religions as the element of sacrifice. It is especially characteristic that in ancient Indian culture, when a follower provided his deity with nourishment and strength by means of a sacrifice, he acquired a certain power over that deity. If the gods have drunk of a man's *soma,* they must stand by him. No doubt a certain element of "sorcery" is at work here, but we should inquire into the more deep-seated reasons for the existence of this phenomenon. It is surely not the result of a metaphysical extension of the economic exchange of value and equivalent value. It could derive, however, from the spiritual significance that all giving has, which goes beyond the actual value of the gift; in accepting the gift, an inner bond is created that cannot be canceled by returning something of the same outward value. Neither is the acceptance of the gift a mere passive material gain; it also involves granting something to the giver. Inherent in the acceptance of a gift is a sense of favor and goodwill quite beyond the actual value of the object given, just as in the giving of the gift. These suprarational overtones broaden the emotional sphere of giving as a sociological phenomenon in a way that prepares it for the sphere of religion to take up and develop further. The Indian idea just cited, insofar as it has not become mechanistic but has retained its inner religious significance, probably requires as its precondition the sociological relationship of giving and accepting; the inner structure of this sociological relationship presents itself to be molded by a general sense of religiousness into a transcendent phenomenon.

Both the parallels and the differences between the social and the religious spheres manifest themselves most directly in what is generally called "duty" in both spheres,] for with the exception of Buddhism and Christianity, this particular aspect always brings together the religious and the social. Throughout the whole of the ancient world and nearly everywhere in the ethnic world, serving the gods is an element of life in the political or family community and is just as much a part of such communities as language. To evade such an obligation would be equivalent to refusing military service or inventing a private language. Indeed, even Buddhism shows evidence of this, though in a negative form, for Buddhism entirely lacks a social dimension. Its ideal is that of the monk's existence, though occasionally it includes elements of sacrifice and suffering for others. This self-denial, however, occurs not for the sake of others but for the sake of the subject and his own salvation. Buddhism teaches complete withdrawal from social life. Self-redemption, according to Buddhism, is no more than a severing of oneself from existence, socially no less than physically. It knows only obligations to oneself; if this happens to include the good of others,

this is the "good of all living beings." This idea contrasts sharply
with the sociopolitical definitions laid down by social obligations in the whole of the classical and non-Christian world, and
also in the larger part of the Christian world.

Buddhism, however, is not a religion. It is a doctrine of salvation that can be attained by the seeker entirely on his own,
by his own desire and reflection, a salvation that will come
upon him readily if he fulfills conditions that are situated only
within the disposition of his soul. Salvation from suffering, the
sole content of Buddhism, requires no transcendent power, no
divine mercy, and no mediator; it is not achieved by the individual but comes to pass as the logical result of the soul's renunciation of all will to live. That there is no correlation here between social and religious obligation, which is otherwise always
present, apart from certain variations within Christian culture,
is attributable to Buddhism's not including the two elements
of this correlation: it does not contain social norms, nor is it a
religion. In all other cases — most visibly in the ancient Semitic,
Greek, and Roman cultures — the religious obligation of sacrifice and prayer, indeed the cult as a whole, is not a personal
matter but is imposed on the individual as a member of a particular group. The group is held responsible for the individual's
religious failings. For precisely this reason, the social life of the
ancient world can proceed entirely in a religious manner: religious dedication, the outward appearance of something that is
merely socially necessary, in fact constitutes an inherent feature
of the fabric of social norms. That social requirements are expressed in religious terms, and that the relationship of the individual to the group is classified as a duty to god, is simply an
outward illustration or objectification of the inner, emotional
motivation already rooted in the social relationships, [or, to be
more precise, in taking on this social form, such inner impulses
become the object or channel for the religious mood.]

The relationship of the devoted child to its parents, of the
enthusiastic patriot to his country, of the fervent cosmopolite

toward humanity; the relationship of the worker to his insurgent class or of the proud feudal lord to his fellow nobles; that of the subject to the ruler under whose control he is, or of the true soldier to his army—all these relationships, with their infinite variety of content, seen from the psychological point of view have a common tone that can be described only as religious. They all contain a peculiar mixture of unselfish surrender and fervent desire, of humility and exaltation, of sensory concreteness and spiritual abstraction; and all of this occurs not only in alternating moods but in a persistent unity that we can rationally comprehend only by breaking it down into such pairs of opposites. This occasions a certain degree of emotional tension, a specific ardor and certainty of the subjective conditions, an inclusion of the subject in a higher order, though he senses it as something inward and personal. These elements of subjective feeling, on which this kind of relationship is based at least in part, both inwardly and outwardly, we can call religious. [This is documented, as if transmuted to concrete substance, in the god's creating or sanctioning of the relations between human beings. For example, gods can be distinguished according to whether they exist for the sake of man's inequality—that is, by legitimating existing inequalities—or for man's equality—that is, whether they are created so that there exists a being before whom all men are equal. But precisely by not impeding the sameness of the transcendent consecration, the divergence of content coincides with the sameness of structure that those ideals in general possess because of their social quality and that prepares them to be enfolded by religious life. Precisely because they are religious, they are endowed with a quality that distinguishes them from relationships based on pure egotism or suggestion, or determined by external forces or even by purely moral demands.

This particular type of emotion can perhaps be described in most cases as piety: the attitude of the soul which becomes religion as soon as it is projected onto certain forms. In the present context it is important to note that the Latin word *pietas* denoted devout behavior both toward other human beings and toward gods. Piety, which might be described as religiosity in its unfixed form, does not necessarily develop into the fixed form of behavior toward the gods—that is, religion. It is characteristic that moods or functions that in their logical essence transcend the soul nevertheless remain within it and do not take on a concrete, objective form. There are loving souls whose entire being and action are determined by the singular softness, warmth, and dedication of love, and yet who never feel love toward a particular person; there are evil hearts whose thoughts and desires are cruel and selfish, though these never assume the concrete form of truly evil deeds; there are persons of an artistic bent whose way of seeing things, of living life, and of shaping their impressions and feelings is entirely artistic, though they never create a work of art. There are also people of a pious nature who never direct their piety toward a god—that phenomenon which is nothing other than the pure object of piety; in other words, there are religious people without a religion. These individuals will be among those who experience and feel the relationships mentioned above with an attitude of religiousness. Of course we call such an attitude religious because the fully developed, concrete, and distinct phenomenon of religion exists, because it has developed from these attitudes alone and has become, as it were, the pure manifestation of the impulses, moods, and needs inherent in the empirical, social material of such conditions of life.

One might imagine that sociological relationships possessing this dynamic quality, [when borne by a life process that is religious as such and is within the bounds of their own sphere,] are actual religious phenomena and take on a life of their own, so to speak, which takes them beyond their immediate social relevance and allows them to create their own "gods" as objects. There are certainly plenty of analogies to this, however far removed in content. For example, it has often been observed that love creates its own object, not merely in the sense that the

erotic urge seeks out its own object to match its desires and fulfill them accordingly, nor in the sense that illusions of love invest
an object with desired qualities that it does not really possess.
But as the object of love, the beloved person is *always* a creation
of the lover, of course with the actual personality traits of the
beloved person, but in essence and idea existing in a completely
different world, totally distinct from the reality of that person
as he or she actually is. One should not confuse these various
imagined qualities of content, however, with the question of
form or essence that is at issue here. The image of the beloved
that has grown from these features may or may not correspond
to reality: the productivity of the loving person in creating his
beloved anew as part of some higher order beyond the physical
sphere does not depend on any such correspondence.

The same applies to the work of art, which—unlike some
mere imitation of reality—upholds its artistic significance quite
independently of whether it derives its content from some existing reality. The work of art issues forth from the inner creativeness of the artist, and it constitutes a work of art insofar as this
creativeness has taken concrete shape within it. Thus it is quite
different, say, from the piece of marble that it represents in the
world of tangible reality, and also quite different from the form
derived from empirical experience. The person who is loved by
another thus belongs to a completely new category of being: he
is the product of love, quite independently of whether the qualities he possesses in the imagination of the person who loves him
are drawn from his real being or are the product of pure fantasy.[3]

These examples are intended to show how the truism that
gods are the product of religiousness (as a quality of the soul) is
part of a broader conceptual scheme. This scheme, as I see it, is
not so obvious. When certain fundamental forces and impulses
of the soul take effect, they create an object for themselves. The

[3] Note that in German *die Person* is feminine.

significance of the object of these functions of love, art, or religiosity amounts to no more than the significance of the functions themselves. [Of course, all such emotional impulses need some concrete content through which to manifest themselves; they must acquire some object.] But this object is assigned a place within the spiritual sphere in being re-created as part of that subjective domain. It is quite immaterial whether the contents that were combined to take on this form existed previously on their own: they become a new phenomenon in their own right. When the relationship of an individual to individuals of a superior order or to a social group, or to the ideal norms or symbols through which the life of the group is expressed, acquires a religious quality — in other words, when sociological facts are subordinated to the religious urge — this, from a functional point of view, is [the same creative activity of a soul by which a "religion" is brought into being, even though it does not culminate in the same degree of differentiation and objectification.] The individual has peopled the world of his religious impulses just as if he were praying to a god; the difference is that in the latter case, the function has achieved a pure form [because it has shed its original, purely socially formed material.]

Whether or not this pure form has been achieved, however, is immaterial as regards the principle under discussion here. The objects of religiosity that man finds in certain social relationships are products of his piety in exactly the same way as the transcendent sphere is such a product. For our present purpose — and perhaps generally — it must remain open to question whether relationships of this kind first existed historically, later developing into religiosity as a transcendent objectification, an abstraction, and a sublimation of the subjective religious element within them, or whether the soul is naturally disposed to direct such feelings and tendencies toward a being external to itself in a purely functional and detached manner, creating an object entirely independently of any previous expression of such feelings in a social or other context, a pure object in which these emotional impulses can find full expression. These reflections concern not the question of historical sequence but purely this issue: whether the religious sphere manifests itself within the entire spiritual complex of the individual's relationships with other people or with a group in the same way as it is experienced in the more obvious and purer manifestations of religion in the normal sense of the word.

### 3. RELIGION AND GROUP UNITY

As I go on to consider in more detail the specific forms of analogies between social and religious behavior, previously discussed from a somewhat general perspective, it will become clear [that such analogies are not to be regarded as some random similarity of unconnected phenomena. Rather I wish to interpret the parallels between the two spheres as follows. The religious category is a spiritual way of living and of experiencing the world, and is a force that searches, acts, feels, and takes hold of the content of existence. This allows it to create an objective world for itself. Religion stands juxtaposed to religiosity, which is in itself a *state* or a spiritual rhythm lacking any object. Among those contents which religiosity pervades or takes control of are the sociological formations whose structure predestines them to be ideal raw material for the development of religious life. If religiosity develops so far as to create its own transcendent forms, such as gods and doctrines of faith (as has happened historically from the very beginning), it will transfer into this transcendent sphere certain forms of its original social contents. These are projected onto the specific religious development; thus they are freed from their social context and are integrated into the transcendent scheme. Or perhaps—and I can suggest this only as a further basis for the above-mentioned "analogy"—one might assume some profound moving forms of spiritual life that take effect in molding both religious and social reality, so that the uniformity of certain phenomena derives from a single, common root that determines their shape.

In light of these reflections] I will first consider religious *faith,* which is generally regarded as the specific essence or substance of religion. The definition of faith especially emphasizes its distinction from what is termed theoretical belief. Belief in this intellectual sense forms part of the same scale as knowledge but is simply lower down on that scale; such belief means holding something to be true for reasons that differ only quantitatively from those which make us claim to *know* something. Metaphysical or epistemological analyses can lead us to regard the existence of God as a plausible, or in some cases, even a necessary hypothesis; then we "believe" in Him just as we believe in the existence of light being diffused through the ether or the atomic structure of matter. If a religious person, however, says, "I believe in God," we immediately sense that something quite different is meant from the acceptance of the truth of His existence. This statement does not merely imply that God's existence is assumed even though it cannot be strictly proved. It implies a certain spiritual relationship to Him, an emotional dedication, an orientation of life toward Him. That the person who makes this statement is convinced of God's existence just as he is of any other reality is only one aspect, or a theoretical expression of the subjective, spiritual condition that the statement immediately describes. The *quality* of the religious soul expressed in this statement is the fountain of youth from which theoretical belief in the existence of God draws its perpetual energy despite all evidence and probabilities to the contrary.

An interesting analogy to "faith" in this sense exists in the sphere of interpersonal relationships; for here, too, we "believe" in somebody. Similarly, this does not mean that we believe in his existence, though it does not specify exactly *what* we believe of or about that person. We describe a specific psychological fact when we "believe in somebody"—the child in its parents, the subordinate in his superior, the friend in his friend, the individual in the nation, the lover in his beloved, the subject in his sovereign. The belief in the reality of specific qualities of such objects of our faith is merely a particularization or consequence of this basic relationship; it implies an attitude of the whole person in regard to the other. Located in a sphere beyond any question of proof or refutation, such belief in a person countless times survives the most objectively founded suspicions and the most obvious revelation of the unworthiness of the person in whom one believes. This is *religious* faith manifesting itself in the relationships between human beings.

The belief in God is the subject's very same state in its orientation to an exterior entity, detached from its empirical object and its relative scale, producing its new object from within itself, and thus raising it to an absolute plane. The sociological and transcendental forms of this faith initially have analogous benefits for the subject. It has rightly been pointed out that faith in some deity creates considerable moral stability and a remarkable sense of elevation above life's ordinariness, quite regardless of whether the object of that faith is real in the objective sense. For faith is a spiritual state: though oriented toward an exterior object, this orientation itself is nonetheless an inner, spiritual quality. Though the soul draws the powers of such elevation from itself [—at least this is how we must view it from a purely psychological point of view—], these powers, by passing through the stage of a faith in God, acquire a more concentrated and more productive form. The soul thus creates from them its own distinct object, and by drawing them back within itself once more can allow them to develop a stature and a strength that otherwise would be unattainable.

This most effective channeling of spiritual energies by religious faith also can occur in one person's belief in another. Belief in a person, even if objectively unjustified, has the enormous advantage of stimulating and combining many powers of the believer's soul which would otherwise have remained subconscious or ineffective. Someone may console us with banal reasons, but in *believing* that he is saying what is best and right we allow him to draw from our soul its own latent forces of consolation. He may give us feeble or inept support in our suffering, but as long as we believe we are being supported, we acquire new courage and strength from our own resources. He may prove something to us with ill-founded arguments, but if we believe that what he says is true, we come to realize the true reasons ourselves. There is no doubt that when we believe in somebody, we invest that person with our own powers; but it is his achievement to have made us discover such powers within us. Finally, we come to the concentrated form of the same process: the individual's belief in himself. This particular type of faith shows most clearly that all its specific contents are merely a series of opportunities for the soul to realize one of its fundamental dispositions. If we believe in another person or in God, we cause the unease and insecurity that it is our universal destiny to feel to be replaced by a sense of stability directed toward these objects. The idea of this person or of God is a tranquilizing force amid the stormy ups and downs of the soul; that we can "rely on them" in a specific situation is the projection of this feeling of security, which characterizes our soul as it forms an image of its object.

This is exactly what is meant by belief in oneself: a very deep-seated sense of calm and stability within the self, expressed in the idea that this self will prove itself and assert itself victoriously in any situation. [Among the ancient Arabs, the belief in oneself appears to have had a particularly interesting combination of societal and religious roots. The life structure of these peoples displays an unlimited degree of self-assurance within the individual, a confident egoism—even aspects that have been described as amounting to self-deification. At the same time, a religion as such could apparently not be discovered, particularly the inevitable cult of ancestor worship. Upon deeper analysis, however, both these phenomena were interpreted according to the ancient Semitic idea that the ancestral line lives on in every descendant and that the tribe—the actual object of religious feeling—was directly present in the blood of every individual. The individual's cheerful self-confidence and unbroken faith in himself thus become, through the idea of heredity, the receptacle into which both the sociological substance and its religious expression flow. The inner certainty that filled the ancient Arab with the knowledge that he was the descendant of such ancestors—a certainty of an entirely religious character and involving a whole system of sacred rights and duties—thus became identical to the sense of certainty with which he believed in himself, or "deified" himself. It is indeed quite usual] for faith in God and belief in himself to give the individual the very same sense of trust in the future, the same capacity to reject a value that has just been proved false and to replace it immediately with some new hope.

Belief in ourselves therefore brings us the same benefits as belief in others—even though it often may lead us astray and exact from us a high price in return for a sense of confidence in anticipation of what we might achieve. Consider how many things we can do only because we believe we can do them, how often a talent is developed to its utmost limit only because we ourselves have set this limit at a yet higher level, how often a person acts in an honorable manner out of a sense of "noblesse oblige," though it is not his previously existing qualities but simply his belief in such qualities that justified this feeling. Practical faith is a fundamental quality of the soul that in essence is sociological, that is, it becomes concretized as a relationship with some being external to the self. That such a relationship is possible between an individual and himself is a result of man's capacity to divide himself into subject and object, to confront himself as he would another person. This capacity has no analogy in any other phenomenon of the world known to us, and it forms the very basis of human nature. That the consequences of different types of faith—whether in oneself, in others, or in God—are related so closely to one another derives simply from the fact that all of these are expressions of the same spiritual tension, varying according to the particular sociological object in question.

The purely social significance of this religious faith beyond that of individual faith has not yet been investigated at all, but I feel sure that without it, society as we know it would not exist. Our capacity to have faith in a person or group of people beyond all demonstrable evidence—indeed, often in spite of evidence to the contrary—is one of the most stable bonds holding society together. Obedience, for example, is frequently based neither on the certain recognition of legality or superiority nor on love or suggestion, but on faith in the power, merit, irresistibility, and goodness of the other. Such faith is not some hypothetical assumption but a unique spiritual bond that develops between human beings.[4] This faith is by no means exhausted in the specific qualities seen to constitute the value of its object: such qualities are relatively random aspects through which the formal mood and orientation toward the other person, the faith in him, become objective and expressible. Its sociological impact, of course, joins with all kinds of other creative forces of knowledge, desire, and affection, whereas in religious faith it presents itself in its pure, self-contained form—an enlargement and elevation of the spiritual quality to an absolute plane, which enable us to perceive its essence within these lower and less pure forms. In the case of faith in God, the process of "believing in a person" has separated itself from its social context and created its object from itself, whereas when faith takes effect in the social sphere, the object it encounters there existed already in other orders. Yet this faith does not become religious only by being extended into the transcendent sphere, which is only a particular measure and means of representation. It is already religious in its sociological [realization; here, too, it is permeated by the energies of formal religion.] In its synthesis of restraint and expansion of the self, of clear-sightedness and blindness, of spontaneous will and dependence, of giving and receiving, faith forms a part of the religious plane onto which the relationships between men are projected.

[4] Compare here Weber's typology of *Herrschaft,* 1978, 212–301.

Even so, it does not take its character solely from the *transcendent* structures inherent in formal religion, though of course it is in formal religion that such faith exhibits its purest form.

One might say that God is the absolute object of faith. It is to God that the religious person allows the entire depth of this spiritual function of faith to crystallize. [This is not disproved but indeed is confirmed if the state of believing is seen to be a fundamental quality of the religious person, even of a person in whom this quality of spiritual being has not yet substantialized itself into the idea of a deity, or no longer does so, but is expressed in a practical, philosophical, or inherently emotional manner.] But it is from this origin that the *absoluteness* of the idea of God derives, from the totality and originality of spiritual energy beyond the relative form it always adopts in specific instances. Here the function of faith belongs to a series of other spiritual qualities that invest the substance of religion with their power through their universality and generality, unprejudiced by any specific content. Thus the Christian God is the absolute God of love. All the specific characteristics of people and things that allow us to realize the possibilities of human love in particular forms give love a specific coloring that allows one love to exist alongside another as instances of the same general concept: love of a different person thus appears as a different type of love. This makes of love an empirical object; even while it remains a process experienced by the individual, to some extent it is a product of both the *individual's* spiritual energies and the nature of their object. Yet because God does not confront the soul as an empirical being with specific, particularized features, He remains the pure product of this spiritual energy of love, in which its variations—otherwise destined to be realized within specific, empirical beings—remain an undivided whole.

In the same sense, God is also the absolute object of man's spiritual search. That restlessness of spiritual life which perpetually seeks to change the objects of imagination finds in Him its absolute goal. The search for God is no longer a search for some

specific object—whatever meaning such a search might have—
but searching as such achieves its goal in God. God is equivalent
to the underlying current of such restless searching, of which
each single instance is only a specific manifestation or part. Because God is "the absolute goal," He is also the absolute goal of
any searching. This demonstrates the deeper significance of the
origin of God as an absolutization of man's urge to impose a pattern of causality on the world. In the empirical sphere, such an
urge is always expressed in specific instances, in which a particular material and its causal form are merged into one. Yet insofar
as the causal urge functions without such specific stimulation by
some empirical object but produces its object as a pure process,
this object will be absolute and universal; as a nonparticularized
energy it can be realized itself only within the causal origin of
being in general.

The Scholastic term for God *ens perfectissimum,* the being
beyond all limitation and specification, is an objectification of
the idea that God originates from what we might call the absolute *within our soul,* from the pure energies deriving only from
the soul itself and not adapted specially to some specific object.
When God is referred to as "love itself," this statement applies to
Him to the extent that it applies to the subject who is engaged
in the spiritual process of love. He is not a single object of love
but derives from the love impulse in its purest form, though this
is never realized as such—the absolute principle of love beyond
any relativization and therefore impurity caused by specific objects. This establishes God's psychological relation with human
interaction in society. All spiritual functions such as love, faith,
longing, and dedication link the subject—as whose spiritual impulses they appear—to other subjects. The relational network
of society is thus woven from the innumerable specifications of
these functions. They might be described as the a priori forms
that by means of individual suggestion generate specific empirical, social-psychic phenomena. Yet when these functions take
effect in their pure form [permeated only by their fundamental

religiousness] and free of objective limitation, then the absolute, religious object becomes their goal and product—[or: the religious element within them is free, endowed only with the form of "a relationship in general"]. In the objective idea of religion, the individual fragments and events of reality are combined in the Divine Being into their absolute, unified whole, a source that reconciles all their irreconcilabilities. In the same way the manifold impulses that link individual souls socially to one another are associated psychologically within the constant, fundamental impulse representing the universal principle of all these different expressions. Such an impulse creates in varying forms the religious relationship between the absolute of humanity and the absolute of being.

Unity is a second concept in which social and religious phenomena display a similarity of form, such that the social form presents itself for religious coloration and the religious form stands as the symbol and absolutization of the social. The bewildering multitude of things, from which only occasionally a causally linked pair of phenomena might emerge, allowed primitive ages only *one* opportunity to sense multiplicity as something unified; this was the social group. The awareness of the unity of the social group must develop from a twofold contrast: first, the hostile demarcation from other groups. Common defense and attack against competitors in securing living space is one of the strongest means of realizing and solidifying the cohesion of group elements. At least as far as the conscious mind is concerned, unity often develops not from within but through external pressure, through the practical needs of the group to assert itself, and largely through the idea—proved in practical deeds more powerfully than by any prevailing authority—that this complex of beings is a unified group. Second, the behavior of the group toward its individual elements gives it the quality of unity. Precisely because these are separate and unattached, free and responsible for themselves, they are felt to be a unified whole. Precisely because the individual feels he is a distinct being must the unifying power joining him to others signal this sense of unity so clearly: whether in that his whole life is permeated with a feeling of dedication toward it or whether in that if he attempts to oppose it, he finds himself in conflict with the entire group. That the freedom of the individual will always try to detach itself from the unity of the group, and that even in the simplest and most naive social entities such unity does not develop as readily as the unity of an organism and its parts—this in particular must have raised human awareness of social unity as a distinct form or energy of being. The organization of primitive collectives in groups of ten clearly reflects a relationship between group elements based on that of the fingers to the hand: each individual member has relative freedom and independent mobility, though the individual is linked firmly to the others in unity of purpose and inseparability of existence. Because all social life is interaction, it is also unity; for what is unity but that many are tied to each other, the destiny of each individual element affecting that of all the others?

The synthesis into a group is the prototype of that subjective and conscious sense of unity which transcends individual personality. Its distinct form is reflected or sublimated in the unity of religious existence, the cohesion of which is provided by the concepts of God. This idea may initially be illustrated by an analysis of the religious group as such. It is well known that in early cultures (including what might be termed noncultures) there were no enduring or organic groups that were not cultic communities. It is particularly interesting to note that during the Roman Empire, when a strong cooperative movement led to the establishment of large numbers of guilds, each guild still had, or appears to have had, its own individual religious cachet. Whether a guild was formed by merchants or actors, litter bearers or physicians, each claimed a particular deity as its protector, had a "genius," or possessed a temple or at least an altar. Not the individual member but the group as such stood under a particular god; this is evidence that such a god expressed the *unity* of the group, that which over and above the individual members held the group together. One might say that *god* was the name given to the social unit, which evoked the specific reaction of piety because and insofar as it was experienced sub specie religionis. [The group's sense of unity was expressed in that the god's interest, in ultimate and absolute terms, related only to the affairs of the community as a whole. Of course the individual might summon demonic powers for his private interests by means of sorcery, but in many cases this was not officially allowed, because the individual was to seek help only within the unity of the group and not at the expense of the community.

No less important is the role of this very social *unity* in early Christianity; indeed, its status came to exceed that of doctrinal values. In the third century, during the controversy over whether those Christians who had been banned from the Church during the persecutions should be readmitted, when the bishop of Rome favored such readmittance, the stricter party in Rome elected for itself a bishop whose qualifications were above reproach. There was no doubt that in a strictly formal religious sense, the inner purity of the Church required that the dissidents should remain barred, or least that the more rigorous-minded should be allowed the possibility of forming their own group. Cyprian, however, was able to have the election of the other bishop declared null and void, because ultimately the requirement of *unity* was felt to be the truly vital interest of the Church. This form of unity had been handed down to Christianity from the spirit of guild life that dominated the Roman imperial period, particularly in its later stages. The very earliest and deepest unity shared by all Christians—that of love, faith, and hope—was in fact more living side by side as like-minded individuals than an organic togetherness that was drawn from the surrounding heathen world, though invested by Christianity with a strength and depth unknown in the heathen sphere.

[Of course, the motive of Christian unity also was reinforced from an entirely different angle: the nature of the new god's *personality.* In the ancient world, the personality of the gods was very much on a human scale; essentially, it did not extend beyond the fragmentary, incomplete nature of human personality. Wherever this was felt to be inadequate and the god was conceived of as an all-embracing and superhuman being, humans turned to a pantheistic perspective—that is, viewed God as possessing no personality. It was Christianity that created the all-embracing God who was at the same time a personal god, displaying the cohesive, unifying strength of this form in the unconditional breadth of His being and deeds. It is in the Christian God that we first encounter this synthesis: the truly superhuman was at the same time personal, just as "society" or the group is the social phenomenon that transcends the individual and yet is not abstract—in fact is perfectly concrete. I would like to believe that this unity of the very highest kind—which must have been far more impressive and more effective because of its personal form, and because of the vitality this gave it, than even the "oneness" of neo-Platonism—was a crucial mainstay for the Church's sense of unity. The converse, however, seems also to apply (though the two ideas do not contradict one another)]: it was its stable sociological structure that gave the Church a sense of absolute, supramundane stability—even of godliness—amid the decline of the ancient world. Christian doctrine did not contain any particular objection to the existence of numerous sociologically independent communities, bound together simply by common teachings and attitudes.

Apparently, however, the power of such a spirit was soon felt to be lacking in strength if it did not exhibit itself as a social-organizational unity. Such unity was not merely a technical means of maintaining the existence and the power of the religion in an external sense; it was the mystical *reality of salvation itself.* Because of its all-encompassing form of unity, the Church appeared as the realization of God's kingdom proclaimed by Jesus. It was glorified as the "City of God," a Noah's Ark incorporating the redeemed community of sacred souls as "the Body of

Christ." There is perhaps no better illustration of the process that these pages seek to describe. The purely empirical-social, historical form of unity is adopted by the subjective religious mood and reveals itself by this means as a reflection of the spiritual impulse: the mystical reality of transcendent unity, the purely religious unification of the world. The specifically religious element appears here as both cause and effect, at least as the ideal expression of that form of social interaction to which we refer as the unity of the group. [A central motif of Mohammed's reforms can be traced back to the same idea, although in a totally different context. Mohammed sought to do away with the tribal principle in order to establish overall national unity. Therefore he decreed that if a murder were committed, no one, on pain of death, was to turn to the tribes but only to God. By God he meant His representatives, who also represented universal law as opposed to tribal law based on private warfare and blood ties. God was thus the unifying metaphysical principle through which the empirical-social fragmentation was to be overcome, both a symbol and the actual juridical agent of sociological unity.]

*One* particular characteristic inherent in the concept of unity lends itself to religious elaboration. In more primitive epochs, the unity of the group was especially enforced or marked by the *lack of feuding and competition* within the group, in contrast to the group's relationship to nonmembers. There is perhaps no other specific domain in which noncompetitive coexistence—the compatibility of goals and interests—was represented so purely and so completely as in religion; the overall pacific unity of the social group appears as a preliminary stage of the same phenomenon. For that pacific unity is only relative at any time: after all, within empirical society it even allows the individual to try to exclude others from achieving the same goals as he, to redress the imbalance between desire and fulfillment even at the expense of his fellows, and to estimate the value of his own actions and pleasures at least in relation to that of others. Almost solely in the domain of religion can individuals' energies develop to their full extent without competing with one another because, as Jesus aptly expresses it, there is room for everyone in God's house. Although the goal is the same for all, everyone has the potential to achieve it, and there is no mutual exclusion; on the contrary, all can join forces in their endeavors. Consider the profound manner in which Holy Communion expresses the idea that religion aims to achieve the same goal for all by employing the same means for all. Also, one might consider in particular the religious festivals that display in the clearest possible concrete form the unity of all those captured by the same religious excitement—from the unsophisticated festivities of primitive religions, where the sense of unity often reaches its climax in the sexual orgy, to that most pure expression of an idea, the pax hominibus, which goes far beyond mere group unity.

The Christian festival of Christmas turns the idea of a peaceful community, which the particularist religions apply only to the group itself, into what is essentially a universal principle. Within any group, the principle of nonaggression applies insofar as the life form of the group depends on it—and clearly that dependence is quite partial and relative. The group religion gives this integrative peacefulness a form that is free of such limitations and that finds expression in religious festivals. The Christian festivals extend this idea of peace further: the individual senses that he is supported in his own mood by the whole of Christianity sharing that feeling with him. This mood in effect breaks down all particularities of group membership. However imperfectly this idea may be realized in historical reality [just as Mohammed could only barely impose in Arabia the theistic-universalistic principle of law mentioned earlier], according to its *idea* the Christian festival performs the unique task of completely removing the barrier that otherwise causes the individual to regard any other existing frame of mind as contradictory and alien. The social principle of nonaggression thus goes beyond its purely internal, sociological character and acquires, in the spirit of such religious festivals, the status of a positive, universal symbol.

In the Jewish and the earliest Christian communities, disputes between members were settled before the congregation or by an arbiter appointed by it. Paul pointed out the contradiction involved in recognizing heathen judges, given that the heathen were regarded as contemptible. From the point of view of peaceful relations, the religious community here appears as a higher form of the inner unity of the group itself. Religion is in a way the essence of peace, the form of group life we call peacefulness into which it solidifies as *one* idea. Clashes might occur between the faithful as private individuals—as tradesmen or as violent persons—but among people seeking to achieve the same religious good, there could be only peace. Thus the social equivalent of this good—the community—was the logical authority to settle social conflicts and bring about peace. The unifying and reconciling power that emanates from religion as a worldview is symbolized by the paramount importance that peaceful coexistence—which to some extent characterizes the inner relations of any group—takes on within the religious group. The latter might be described as the transition through which sociological unity [—insofar as this manifests itself in a life that is religious in a functional sense—] is transposed into the absolute unity of the idea of the deity. This progression has another stage, which in many respects is typical of the pre-Christian era. In this stage the deity is not an entity *separate* from the individual and his sphere, but is included in the latter; it is an element of the immediate totality of life on which the individual depends.

In ancient Judaism, for example, on the occasion of the sacrificial slaughter the god participates in the feast, so that the feast is more than simply a matter of paying tribute to the god.[5]

[5] Simmel presents an early distinction between magic and religion in this paragraph.

Everywhere the god is a relative of his worshippers. Wherever the god is the tribal father, king, or indeed in any sense god of *a particular* social group or city, while other gods of equally unquestioned existence are peculiar to other groups—in all such cases, the god is the supreme *member* of the community. He lives as part of the social unit and at the same time is its very expression. Of course, as the latter he stands apart as a distinct entity from the individual group members, although in the same way as the pater familias is an integrative symbol of the family, or as the sovereign represents the sum total of his subjects. The deity has the same remarkably complex sociological status: as one of the members of a group that becomes crystallized in these members, providing the integrative force that binds together all other members, and yet in a certain sense distinct from this unified whole as an independent and counterbalancing force. [This is why it has been possible to state, particularly in reference to the facts of the ancient Semites' religion, that a supernatural being is not necessarily a god—a claim I also believe is justified. The primitive peoples' tendency to the fantastic easily led to the creation of demons as explanations of reality. Initially such a being exists only *for itself*: it does not become a god until it has gathered a group of worshipers around it, just as a god can be reduced to a mere demon if he loses his worshipers. Only when some kind of regulated relationship with a community is developed—and the form of this relationship is modeled on the human community in question—does such a demonic being cease to exist merely for itself and become a living and active *god* for man.] For this reason the particular god always has a form that is appropriate to the form of the relevant society. As long as Semitic communities were based on kinship, the god of the Jews, the Phoenicians, and the Canaanites was the father, and the followers were his children. As soon as the social group became a political unification of various peoples, however, the god had to take the form of a king. For technical reasons, as it were, his status had to become much more abstract and more detached so that he could remain both within the group as a member and above it as deity.

Yet even if the emphasis is the deity's elevation above the rest of the group, it does not mean that the vital relationship between the deity and the social form of the group is interrupted. In Greece and Rome, where the monarchy was overpowered by the aristocracy at an early stage, an aristocratic order also imposed itself on religion, with a hierarchy of several gods of equal standing—a pure and distinct image of the form of the group's social unity, devoid of its commercial, tribal, and political interests. In Asia, by contrast, where the monarchy remained powerful for a much longer time, the religion tended to center on a god with monarchic power. Indeed, the strength of tribal unity that dictated the social life of the ancient Arabs itself prefigured monotheism. Even the unifying power of religion in its transcendence of gender differences can be observed in a particular type of religion. An important factor in the social life of the Syrians, the Assyrians, and the Lydians was the psychological blurring of gender differences. This finds expression in deities that combine such different features within themselves: the half-male Astarte, the male-female Sandon, the sun god Melkarth, who exchanges gender symbols with the moon goddess.

This is not merely an illustration of the trivial idea that man projects himself onto his gods; that idea is a truism that requires no proof. We must rather appreciate that gods are not simply an idealization of individual characteristics—strength, moral or even immoral qualities, the likes and needs of individuals—but that interindividual forms of social life often determine the content of religious images. [Man's religious impulse, which also pervades empirical reality, seizes on the form of this reality as it presents itself and carries it into the transcendent sphere; for this sphere is the location of man's spiritual yearnings, just as empirical space is the location of our sensory impressions. One might also say that the process of social unification causes a religious reaction: the former contains inherent shaping forces that lead the human being beyond his immediate empirical existence and impose mystical interpretations on all social life that transcends the individual. In any case, such forces draw life toward our inner contexts, where life can generate precisely this kind of religious reaction. Historically speaking, such a religious reaction will be all the more probable, the more these ties have not yet been worn and broken down by the differentiation and individuation of social elements.]

#### 4. RELIGION AND THE DEVELOPMENT OF THE SELF

The social relationship just described, involving a sense of being both on the inside and on the outside of society, does not apply only to the leader but to every member of society; and just as this fundamental sociological form prefigures the deity, so it also molds the religious person. That the individual's sense of social belonging to his group always entails a mixture of enforcement and personal freedom, as alluded to earlier, now reveals itself as the most profound formal link between social and religious life.

The real practical problem of society lies in the relationship of its forces and patterns to the independent lives of the individuals within it. Of course, society lives only through the existence of individuals; this, however, does not exclude a great many conflicts between the two. First, the specific form "society," [to which individuals have given the social elements of their being,] acquires its own agents and organs, which confront the individual like an alien body, with demands and obligations. Second, there is a latent potential for conflict [in that society is represented both in and by the individual, as it were]. Man has the capacity to split himself into different parts and to feel that one such portion is his real self, although this one part clashes with other parts and competes for the determination of his actions. This capacity often puts man—insofar as he is and feels himself to be a social being—in a conflicting relationship with those impulses and interests of his self which are not related to society. The conflict between society and individual thus extends into the individual as the struggle between elements of his being.[6] The most profound and most comprehensive clash between individual and society seems to me not to be limited to one particular aspect of life but to derive from the general form of individual life. Society tends toward a total organic unity, of which each of its members forms a part. The individual is expected to invest all of his resources, if possible, in the performance of this specific function, and accordingly adapts himself in the best possible way to fulfilling this function.

The individual's own sense of unity and wholeness, however, comes into conflict with these demands of society. The individual not only wishes to play his part in perfecting social harmony and integration; he also wants to find inner harmony, to develop the whole range of his abilities regardless of which constellation of these abilities best suits the interests of society. This is probably the essence of the individual's assertion of his freedom in the face of social bonds. Such freedom cannot be a question merely of making something gratuitous happen, independent of societal determination. The meaning of freedom is absolute self-responsibility, which we desire, but possess only when our actions are the pure expression of our own personality, when our self, uninfluenced by any other authority, speaks through our actions. We wish the peripheral sphere of our existence to be determined by its center, not by the external forces with which it is inextricably bound up, and which of course become motivating impulses within us even though we often sense that they do not grow naturally from within us. Freedom of the individual that invests him with true responsibility for his actions will cause all his actions to form an organic whole that

[6] Compare the concepts of "I" and "me" in the writings of George Herbert Mead.

fundamentally conflicts with the higher unity that integrates him and commands his dependence. If man's freedom and his subordination to societal forces clash like two conflicting demands, this problem appears to be transformed from a question of law to a question of fact when applied to the religious sphere.

This question is rooted in the depths of all religions, however undeveloped and subconscious, conditional and fragmentary it may remain: whether the divine will on which the world process depends determines the human being totally, as it does the world process, such that he has neither freedom nor responsibility, or whether we have an inner independence before God that allows us both freedom and responsibility but releases us from the all-embracing grasp of divine power. The second alternative is really inconsistent with the concept of an almighty God. Only seemingly can this question be answered by logical considerations or by reference to revelation. In reality it is the conflict between man's *yearning* to stand independent of even the highest authority of existence and to find the meaning of his life within himself, and his other yearning to be included in the divine scheme of things and to be a part of its greatness and beauty—[though this can be achieved only as a reward for selfless dedication and subordination to the whole]. The dignity of individual freedom, the strength or defiance of self-responsibility that takes on itself the full consequences of sin, and clashes with the relief of the self by divine power, the alleviation or even ecstatic melting away in the knowledge that one is part of an absolute whole and all its powers, unconditionally borne up and permeated by its spirit. It is quite clear that the self's sense of life is confronted with the same problem both in social and religious terms, and that these are only two forms or variations of a dualism that determines our soul, our destiny, and their very root.

[If this relationship of the part to the whole appears to be of a rather substantial character, perhaps it can be described in a more functional manner as follows: in all the individual's social ties—in the broadest sense of the term—an element of obligation and an element of freedom can be observed, however specific its content and however consistent its form. Even in the face of the most merciless coercion, the securing of our freedom always depends on the price we are prepared to pay for it. Even in a state of complete freedom, the degree to which we are still conscious of some obligation will depend on how far we are able to comprehend the true structure of the relationship in question. But freedom and obligation perhaps are no more than categories into which we dissect the nature of a relationship not directly definable in other terms, which we view therefore as some combination of the two—even though these categories themselves are as difficult to quantify as any other. Yet this constant intertwining of freedom and obligation, even if it is only symbolic, is one of the social formative processes that is ideally suited to adopting and shaping fundamental religiousness, which otherwise exists merely for itself. For within this spiritual state, I believe it is possible to discern—on close inspection—a harmony of freedom and obligation. These are not meant here as types of relationship to real authorities but as the pure tension and release of the soul, a hovering between boundless extension of the self and the confining constriction of life that cannot find release, a combination of power and powerlessness that cannot be defined in logical terms. The self-contained state of religious being, that unity which knows no otherness, finds a form of expression in the interplay between freedom and obligation as displayed in empirical human relationships; by describing this religious state as a duality, it is as if we were giving it the words with which it can describe itself, even though these words belong to a foreign language. In the categories of freedom and dependence, which religion as a spiritual quality seems to presage, it can pour forth its energies to generate a relationship to the absolute. The state of religious being would not be capable of groping toward the absolute unless it could find the contents capable of being assigned a religious form.

Let us return now to the interplay of freedom and obligation as a form of conflict: the individual desiring to be a self-contained whole, while the overall unity accords him only a subordinate status.] In purely conceptual terms a solution is possible here, namely a structure of the whole that is oriented toward the independence and the stable unity of its elements, a structure indeed that such independence and unity make possible. The conflict would then cease to be a logical one in which each side represents an a priori exclusion of the other; instead it would become merely a practical conflict that could be settled by rearranging the elements without changing them in essence. Such an outcome is conceivable at least in sociological terms as the ideal societal constitution on which actual forms of society would seek to model themselves. The perfect society would then be that which consists of perfect individuals. Society lives its life in a peculiarly hybrid state of abstractness and concreteness; each individual gives it certain of his parts or energies, so that it grows from the contributions of its individual members, who form or seek to form their existence according to their own distinct pattern. Conceivably, however, this supraindividual entity might be such that it accepts constructive contributions only from individuals who are centered harmoniously within themselves. It might be that the life of the societal whole, otherwise raised above the constituent individuals and causing by this separation and autonomy the conflict between *its* form and that of individual existences, now would return to the level of the individual lives. We might perceive a certain abstract grandeur in the idea that a state or any social unit develops its own conditions and patterns of life, forcing the individuals to perform certain tasks and imposing patterns on their lives with abstract detachment and indifference, though these patterns might bear no relation to the principles of the individuals' own being. Such an idea may appear grandiose in its abstractness and yet disclose its provisional quality as an attempt to make a virtue of necessity.

By contrast, it may be utopian, though not inconceivable, that an integrated and uniform structure of societal elements

might develop in which these elements display the fulfillment
and satisfaction of their existence, growing harmoniously while
pursuing their own paths of development. In the inorganic
world this would be a contradiction: no house can consist of
houses, no tree can be made up of trees. In organic nature, however, this contradiction is lessened by the fact that the cell of
an organism has a kind of life of its own, which in some way
is analogous to that of the whole organism. The soul also may
succeed — at least in principle — in achieving what is otherwise
impossible: to be a whole and yet part of a whole, and thus assist in building a supraindividual order in complete individual
freedom. The case of religion, however, is surely quite different
in this respect. After all, society has an interest only in the specific qualities and actions of its members; if these serve societal
unity and perfection, society will not object that the individuals
also gain a free and harmonious life from them. In confronting
God, however, there is more at stake than specific details or the
mere concordance or opposition of our actions in relation to His
will; what is at stake is the principle of freedom and independence in its purely inner meaning. The issue here is whether man
is essentially responsible for himself or whether God operates
through man as if man were an organ without a self; whether
self-oriented human will as an ultimate purpose is justifiable in
religious terms, even when its content does not deviate from
divine will, or whether the sole motivation of life can be only
inclusion in a divine scheme, even when that scheme does not
conflict with the pursuit of self-interest; whether human life is
thus fundamentally denied the possibility of any self-perfecting
form or autonomous organization. Here again it is quite clear
that the relationship in the religious sphere represents an elevated and absolutized form of its social equivalent. The conflict
between the whole and the fragment that itself strives to be a
whole, between the freedom of the single element and its incor-
poration within a higher unity, is within society only an outward
and, as it were, technically insoluble problem. As a relationship

to the deific being that fills the world, however, it [the conflict] is a deep-rooted and fundamentally irreconcilable disharmony.

[I shall now analyze a more specific aspect of this type of relationship between the social and the religious spheres.] According to its stage of development, society compels its individuals to division of labor. The more various the tasks different people perform, the more urgently does one person depend upon the other; the more stable is the sense of unity they achieve by exchanging products; the greater is the satisfaction in fulfilling each other's needs and complementing each other in character and personality. The justification for drawing a parallel between society and the living unit of the organism derives from the concept of the division of labor—in a very general sense, not simply in economic terms—and from the special functions of the elements that link them together. One fills the space that another has left free; one dedicates itself to satisfying others' needs because others have satisfied *its* needs. The division of labor is the corrective to competition: the latter is the mutual displacement of individuals because they pursue goals in which not all can share. The division of labor, on the other hand, is a process through which individuals make space for each other, a harmonization in which each one seeks to test his capabilities in a domain and a manner that are different from others; the division of labor aids societal unity to the same extent that competition undermines it. The freer scope and the more specialized development that it grants the individual, however, run the risk of deteriorating into atrophy as soon as it coincides with the antagonistic principle of competition, as is increasingly the case in the development of modern culture. This is the case because, in the vast majority of cases, the division of labor is only a differentiation of the means and methods for achieving a goal that is still common to all of those involved in achieving it: public favor, a share in the resources and pleasures available, the acquisition of superior status, power, and renown. These universal values remain subject to competition. The division of labor generally is not capable of banishing competition definitively by introducing new societal goals but can only deflect and divert it temporarily.

In addition, because of the increasing density of populations and their needs, every new instance of an outstanding accomplishment is adopted immediately by a large number of competitors, so that precisely at the point where competition should disappear, a focal point for new competition comes into being. The game thus begins again; that is, further competition forces a more specialized division of labor. As a result, the individual is pressed into a one-sided mold of exclusive, specialized activity, and all the energies he possesses that are not thus employable are stunted in their growth: such is the flaw of all very complex cultures. At the root of this process is the relationship described above: the interest and the life of society force the individual into a subexistence that conflicts completely with his personal ideal of his self as a harmonious and balanced whole. Division of labor in its extreme form, as endlessly increasing competition, reveals itself as a form that serves society's close-knit inner unity and the fulfillment of its needs. Yet it pays the price for this perfection of societal balance with the imperfection of the individual, the unnatural forcing of his energies into a specialized activity that leaves much of the enormous potential of these energies to waste away.

The religious sphere reflects this relationship of the individual to the higher order in characteristic angles of refraction. According to the most profound subjective purpose of religion, namely the soul's path to salvation, it invests all individual souls with a certain equality in which each has the same relationship to the absolute. The souls' sense of mutual belonging and common interest derives from this equality, not from differences whose harmonization allow a common goal to be achieved. Where a large number of individuals "call out to God"—providing that each one of them has a direct relationship to his God—one might say that the only added effect is the bodily reinforcement of their prayer. Their number does not create some new form that finds an otherwise inaccessible path to God's ear; it merely adds to the total and perhaps impresses God more by its quantity than does the faintly echoing voice of the single individual. This type of religious relationship precludes any essential differentiation; the perfection of the whole does not depend on individuals' pursuing different activities, as in the case of the social phenomena discussed above, but on the uniformity of the individuals' involvement. The perfection of each one singly does not require another's distinctive contribution. The force linking the faithful here lies solely within the deity itself, insofar as each individual is dedicated to it and is accepted by it.

[In Christianity there are underlying impulses that allow personality and fellow feeling to take on a new and distinctive quality. Christianity has taken a great step forward toward a spiritual socialization: the personal, private nature of the spiritual sphere where each individual is alone with himself, the subjective quality of all action, is no longer merely individualistic and solipsistic but is now brought out of isolation and set into relationship to all other people. Through encountering all others in God, and through being placed before the forum of the invisible church, the individual is no longer left alone with this private sphere. The idea of the invisible church, on the one hand, and—because God is father of all—the symbolic kinship of all Christians on the other, is the most magnificent attempt— however partially it has succeeded in the historical development of Christianity—to achieve unity without employing the means of differentiation. This synthesis of a sense of personality and a sense of solidarity, achievable only in this way, perhaps finds its most profound expression in the idea, occasionally encountered, that each individual is in some way responsible for the sins of the others. Of course this idea is not unknown to non-Christian mysticism, but in the latter it is always based on pantheism and therefore does not embrace the principle of personality. By contrast, the Christian constellation of this synthesis seems to me to indicate a particularly profound and powerful sense of personality—possibly even to the extent that this sense of personality is held to be of limitless and unrestrained power, though in total rejection of any isolating, individual particularization of mankind. This powerful motif shows that the inner "socialization" of Christianity does not in any sense need to denote the herdlike unity of some mechanistic psychocommunism; rather it involves an *organic* unity whose hallmark is that it does not employ the means for unifying the physiological and external social organization, namely that of differentiation.]

I shall now consider one type of a very specific division of labor within the religious domain, namely the priesthood. Buddhism has the clearest view of the sociological origins of priests: there, the religious functions originally practiced by each individual were transferred to particular individuals who took on these functions on behalf of the others—just as the monarchy originated when people elected somebody specifically to punish malefactors, giving this person a share of their harvest in return, instead of taking personal revenge if they were wronged, as they had done previously. [The same phenomenon is known to have occurred in the development of Christianity. The officers of the early Christian church were full members of ordinary life; its bishops and presbyters were bankers and cattle breeders, physicians and silversmiths. They were simply *exemplary citizens* who were required to remain at the level of the community itself, because others were supposed to follow their example. Every member of the community was a "limb of Christ," so these individuals were by no means differentiated from the rest as invested with some superior power.

Only when the communities became considerably larger and when, with this increase in quantity, the differences in quality between individual members increased, did the organization demand centralization and greater power for the highest official. This sociological necessity finally turned him into a ruler, compared with whom the layman was without rights and

entirely dependent in the religious sense. It is important to recognize that this centralization caused the development of an entirely new form of religious life. Man's religious need—the salvation of the soul—remains the same both before and after. The
way in which this inner religiousness manifests itself, and which
type of "religion" it outwardly generates, appears to be entirely
dependent on the sociological possibilities that confront it. It
does not create a transcendent sphere by abstracting the spirit of
empirically existing social forms, so to speak, but itself creates
a sociological sphere that reflects back on the spiritual constitution of the inner religious state. The differences mentioned,
which circumstances impose on the societal structure, are reflected in differences in the subjective domain. For it is quite
clear that religion has a completely different inner significance
for a person whose ultimate salvation depends on a priest than it
would if it depended on God alone; similarly, the subjective religiousness of the priest or monk will be different from that of the
layman. In this particular case, the relationship of the inner religious state to the sociological formations it permeates—because
these have become part of the church—no longer leads upward
to the transcendent sphere but leads backward and inward to the
fully developed form of religion that is shaped by the *soul*.]

The priesthood as a product of the division of labor represents religion in a distinctive sublimation, an abstract synthesis
of the formative powers of practical-social phenomena. In this
synthesis, the division of labor is based on two motifs: on the one
hand, the variety of personal dispositions that invest one individual with the ability and the urge to do something of which
another is not at all capable; on the other hand, the specialized
needs of society as described above, the necessity of exchange
and successive competition. The former motif determines the
division of labor more as *terminus a quo,* the latter as *terminus
ad quem.* From the standpoint of personal qualities, the former
is derived from the distinctiveness and irreplaceability of each
individual, the latter from the essential sameness of all people,

which becomes differentiated only as a result of the demands and goals set by external forces. In the person subject to any division of labor a characteristic synthesis takes place between a sense of vocation from within, based on individual qualification, and a predestination by external influences that assign the individual a particular task even if his talents are very moderate. These two impulses thus derive from different sources and in practice are frequently in discord with one another. The urgings of inner vocation are often deflected and obstructed by the demands and concerns that transcend the individual's own life. Conversely, that which objective powers and situations demand of us is often far removed from our own disposition, and from what we are *truly* capable of doing.

Through the *ordination* of priests, the priesthood transforms this often unsuccessful synthesis into an ideal form that immediately precludes disharmony. In the ordination of a priest, a spirit that exists in mystical objectivity is transferred to the candidate, so that he is its receptacle or representative. In principle, his own personal qualification for the priesthood is of no importance. Ordination means that the individual is accepted into a suprasubjective order and is directed by a guiding force that embraces his personality. Yet these influences direct the individual as from within. The individual concerned is not given this task because he is naturally predestined for it (although this also can play a part and accounts for certain variations among those who are admitted to office), nor on the basis of a *chance* that he might be predestined for his office, whether or not this is actually the case. In fact, the ordination itself creates the particular qualification needed for the task in question, because it invests the individual with the *spirit*. The saying has it that if God assigns a person a post, He also gives him the good sense to go with it; the ordination of priests is the perfect realization of this idea. The randomness in the societal division of labor, by which the subject's particular natural abilities are matched with the external shaping powers bearing down on him, finds an a priori substitute in ordination, the transferral of the spirit. In ordination the suprapersonal scheme into which the individual passes, claiming him for its particular services, imposes on him an essentially new character and makes him entirely suitable for his office. Here again the religious category represents the ideal, reflecting the sociological forms as in a clear mirror that cancels out their contradictoriness and mutual invalidation.

Let us return to the social type of religiousness mentioned above: the complete uniqueness of the individual confronted with his God and thus apparently knowing no differentiation, for all are to achieve the same goal by the same means, with no higher unity bestowing any special, distinctive powers on individuals. This type presents a very fundamental problem, precisely because of the individualistic form of the salvation of the soul. By the idea of the soul's salvation I do not simply mean a state reached by humankind beyond the grave; it is the fulfillment of the soul's ultimate desires, the achievement of absolute spiritual perfection, possible only as an agreement between itself and its God. The question of whether a soul that has found salvation might be in a mortal body or in some heavenly domain is quite superficial, and is as insignificant as if one were to ask in which house we are to meet our destiny. Of all the many possible meanings of this ideal, one seems to me to be particularly important: that the soul's salvation is no more than the unfolding or external realization of what—to a certain extent—we already are in our spiritual self. One might say that what we *ought* to be permeates the imperfect reality of our actual self as a latent ideal. Nothing needs to be added or appended to the soul from outside; only a flaky shell must be cast off to reveal that true core of its being, which previously had been obliterated by sin and error. It is peculiar to this ideal of the soul's salvation as conveyed by the Christian faith—although quite fragmentary and deflected by very different tendencies—that this carving out of our personality, its liberation from all that is not itself, this realization of the conception and law of the self, is the same as being obedient to *divine* will. The salvation that the soul is commanded to seek by its God would not be its own, but would be color-less and spiritually alien, if the path toward it were not already mapped out within the soul itself like a still invisible ideal, and if it were not gained through a process of discovery of the self. [This is illustrated perfectly in a story about a miracle-working Galician rabbi named Meir. He is supposed to have said to his pupils: "If the Lord asks me in the hereafter: 'Meir, why did you not become Moses?' I will reply: 'Because I am only Meir, Lord.' And if he goes on to ask me: 'Meir, why did you not become Ben Akiba?' I will also reply: 'Because I am simply Meir, Lord.' But if he asks me: 'Meir, why did you not become Meir?' what shall my answer be then?"]

This interpretation of the soul's salvation as the deliverance, the demystification, so to speak, of the soul's essence, an essence that is always present but is mixed with alien, impure, and fortu-itous elements—such an interpretation seems to clash with one particular basic precept of Christianity: the equal ability of *every* individual to achieve ultimate salvation, the dependence of this salvation on accomplishments that from the very outset are not inaccessible to anyone. There is room for all in God's house be-cause the greatest that can be achieved by any human is, at the same time, the least that is to be expected of him and there-fore in principle cannot be denied anybody. But if salvation is to consist of nothing but that each and every soul should express and become totally immersed in its innermost being, the pure image of itself whose contours are imposed as an ideal form on its mortal imperfection—how, then, is it possible to recon-cile the infinite variety of souls in their stature and depth, their breadth and limitations, their brightness and darkness, with the sameness of religious success and the equal worthiness before God? How indeed, when this concept of salvation singles out as its very vehicle those elements of a person's being which are most individual and which distinguish him most from others? It is true that the difficulty of reconciling equality before God with the immeasurable diversity of individuals has led to that uniformity of religious achievement which has turned much of Christian life into mere schematism. Christians have failed to take into account all the individualism inherent in the Christian concept of salvation, the idea that each person should make the most of *his own talent;* they have been demanding of everyone a single, uniform goal and identical behavior instead of asking every person simply to give of himself. Anything that is globally uniform must remain superficial to an individual's personality. That oneness which unites the faithful, the equality of perfect souls, consists only in the permeation of each individual's outward actions with the idea that is peculiar to himself; yet the actual context of each idea may be worlds apart. Jesus indicates in several instances how much he values the diversity of individual potential within human beings, but at the same time how little this affects the equality of the final outcome of life.

[Seen in this light, the idea of equality before God is far less clear and less simple than might generally be thought. The communist idea has rightly been rejected, namely that all differences in value that we feel exist between individual souls disappear before God, and that each person has exactly the same validity as any other. What is actually meant is something negative, namely, that none of the value scales that are external to religion but that tend to dominate the mortal order apply before God. This in fact is no different from the idea of "equality before the law," which does not mean that a person who breaks a minor police regulation is treated in the same way as one who robs and murders. It simply means that the personality features of offenders that are irrelevant to their legal position should not have any effect on the verdict. Just as this equality before the law allows every legal inequality to eventuate in its juridical consequences unhindered, so the differences in religious value among men would not be demonstrated in a clear and unhindered way if there were to be no equality before God.

I do not deny, however, that the idea of equality before

God has another, more obscure significance that appears to clash with this logically and ethically clear sense. It may sound absurd, but it is not entirely superficial to believe that a "mechanical" equality of value exists that makes a minor scoundrel equal to a great hero. This idea has frequently had currency—not always in its strictest sense but as a general principle or tendency. It is a metaphysical motif that seems to me to make sense: that the soul as such possesses an eternal value, in comparison with which all the variations in which it manifests itself in the course of life are trivial and irrelevant. From any earthly perspective, whether intellectual, ethical, or aesthetic, this equality cannot apply, for here all value must be expressed in terms of "more" or "less." Just as we can accept that any evaluation is based solely on differences and their relativity, with the soul as the value-free basis that is taken for granted, we also can accept the reverse: that all spiritual being is of equal value regardless of individual qualification, at least from a religious viewpoint that dispenses with such categories of relativity.

This, however, presents us with a fundamental difference, not between empirical and religious evaluation, but between features of human character that display their distinctiveness in both the empirical and the transcendental spheres. Modern socialism also rejects mechanical egalitarianism and advocates only "justice": that is, a social order in which—unlike in the present one—every performance is rewarded exactly according to its merits. In other words, the accepted *differences* between members of society are matched by different reactions in society. In spite of such explanations, I believe that socialism will always draw its energies from those people whose mental makeup leads them to believe in the a priori ideal of absolute equality. Whether one regards the idea as unjust, unclear, or intellectually and practically unrealizable, there are indeed people of this nature, whose ultimate concept of social order must be expressed as assigning absolute equality to everything that bears a human face. Even in Rousseau and the whole of eighteenth-century liberal idealism this conviction was powerful; it stood in irreconcilable conflict with the opposing idea that the value of every human being can be expressed only as being greater or lesser than that of others. Therefore, I continue to believe that in accordance with our perception of human differences, our sense of equality before God goes in both directions; and in Christianity conviction is certainly not lacking that all souls are ultimately destined to acquire equal salvation. Nor does such radical spiritual egalitarianism hesitate to recognize the truth of the principle of equality to those who are equal, inequality to those who are different, because no practical consequences derive from the belief that souls as such do not know definitive inequality.

The only way to develop this idea somewhat more precisely seems to be as follows: one cannot deny the differences between individual souls, for even if this were only a question of outward *appearances,* the *differences* in the outward appearances would require our attention. Therefore the only possible remaining standpoint is that differences are not to be seen as differences in value but as differences in nature. And this is conceivable, as mentioned earlier, only in the sense that empirically given differences in value do not affect our ultimate being and that anything in a human being that is described as bad, evil, or base is merely a *distraction* from the individual's true character. These are *negations* that must be overcome in either earthly or transcendent life to allow the soul to reveal its genuine inner nature as still distinctive and incomparable and yet, by divine standards, equal to all others and an aspirant with them to the same salvation.]

This concept of salvation suggests that man's religious character can take a multitude of forms. Yet such religious differentiation is not a division of labor as such because each individual can achieve complete salvation for himself, albeit in his own particular way. Even so, it retains the sense of a division of labor as an inner impulse: the particularity of each existence, the feeling that the individual is called on to perform a task that no one else can do for him and to occupy a position that has been set aside for him alone. Here we see once again how religious existence adopts the forms of social life and imposes a certain stylized pattern on them, as it were. These are fundamental categories of the soul, which manifest themselves now in the practical-social sphere, now in the religious domain; [or one might say that the subject matter of sociology offers the religious being a channel through which to take shape. For the religious content of life] is less intertwined with random conflicting and heterogeneous social interests and underpins the fragmentary nature of the empirical order with the ideal of the absolute. This religious content appears as a pure and consistent representation of these fundamental spiritual categories, which in themselves are inconceivable. The religious form of a relationship or event presents itself as the purified image of its social equivalent, cleansed of error and of its rough and rudimentary nature.

Art similarly has been described as the immediate, concrete representation of the primal images of man's being, whereas in fact it is only one particular form in which such images manifest themselves, just as the form of empirical existence is such a manifestation. It is simply that certain ways of representing such primal images seem to possess an inner purity and perfection that give them the appearance of faithful imitations of the absolute, though of course they are no more faithful than other such realizations of that idea. The factor that enables religion to represent the distinctive individuality and the coexisting diversity within humanity in a *single* harmonious realm is its absence of competition. In the social sphere, on the one hand, competition promotes the differentiation of individuals and can bring about a wonderful development toward close integration and harmony. On the other hand, competition discourages maintaining such harmony, and its driving force allows the decay of individuality into one-sidedness and blatant disharmony. The difference between the ultimate goal of religion and that of any social activity is that in the case of religion, no aspirant need abandon the quest if another person is successful; it distinguishes itself from competition in that it does not need to extend the development of individuality beyond the point that is defined by the needs and ideals of individual uniqueness. Thus, where individual differentiation in this religious sense manifests itself, it is less acute and less exaggerated than its social equivalent often is, and for this very reason it presents a purer and more perfect counterimage of the latter.

### 5. THE INTEGRATIVE POTENTIAL OF RELIGION

If we start with the idea of a "kingdom of God" and assume that the differentiation of souls constitutes the unity of such a kingdom, where—from a higher perspective—the individual elements merge together to form such unity, it becomes clear that God ultimately represents the absolute unity of existence. This is the only way of expressing this relationship between the deity and both the spatial-empirical world and the heterogeneous multitude of souls. But what does this concept actually mean? It could be interpreted in the pantheistic sense, according to which God is the whole of reality. Both the grain of dust and the human heart, both the sun and the bud that blooms in the sun's rays—all are of the same value, all are equal parts or revelations, the emanations or manifestations of divine being. To state that this being lived *within* them would already express a certain separation and would involve the independent existence of some exterior sphere that is not God. But according to this view, every fragment of existence *is* God; for this reason every fragment is in essence and in truth identical to every other. Pantheism dispenses with both the separateness and the independence of things. There can be no question of interaction here: the metaphysical, essential unity is literal, unlike that of the organism or of society, whose elements possess unity only through an exchange of energies. This God of pantheism, however, is not the God of religion, for he lacks the distinctness or separateness that man needs in order to project his inner religiousness. Love and alienation, dedication and godforsakenness, the sense of intimacy or distance in a relationship: all of these are potentially inherent in the spiritual life of religion but become inapplicable as soon as every single point or moment is included within the unity of the divine. This unity therefore must have another meaning if it is to be the object of religion, for it cannot be identical to the material reality of the world.

Apart from this concept of unity that cancels out all the heterogeneousness of existence, that makes such unity identical to all of its individual elements by making it identical to God, there is only *one* other idea: the idea, mentioned earlier, of unity as interaction. This is what we might describe as *one* being whose elements are linked through their mutually interactive forces; the destiny of each is related to that of all others. Apart from the pantheistic interpretation, this is the only conception of unity that human thought is able to apply to the world, and that idea manifests itself symbolically in the organism and the social group. God conceived of as the unity of existence can be nothing other than the agent of this interlinking, this interaction between things. Man's fundamental religious energy filters or crystallizes this unique being from the complex interaction of the world—the point at which all life forces are as one, where all exchanges of energy converge, and through which all relationships pass. Only in this sense of unity can the God who is such unity be the object of religion, because only in this way can God be an entity *separate* from the individual, both exterior to him and above him. This god of the most highly developed stage of religion is prefigured by the gods who present themselves to us as the representation of the forces at work in the social group, even in the case of polytheistic religions, where each god stands for only one specific domain.

Outside Christianity, the gods are—if not exclusively, at least partially or in one sense—the transcendent images of group unity, in this very sense of a unifying and socializing *function*. Of course, this function is by no means easy to analyze: it has the

same effect as when the king declares "L'état, c'est moi." Here
again, this statement does not denote some pantheistic identifi-
cation but merely indicates that the forces that shape and mold
society are centered on the king, or that his person represents
the equivalent or the sublimation of the dynamic unity of the
state. The process of imagination by which God comes to be
the unity of all things is the same as that by which it is said that
He *is* love, goodness, or justice—a further aspect of the definition of divine unity attempted earlier. It is less a question of
His *having* these qualities than of His *being* them. Man's religious
spirit tends to remove the object it creates for itself beyond all
empirical relativity and confinement into the sphere of the absolute, for only in this way can it achieve the depth and breadth
to match the profundity of religious inspiration within his soul.
Yet every specific quality conceived of in absolute terms devours
its possessor to some extent and leaves behind none of the actual
state of being with which it was associated originally. Just as a
person who is filled with some infinitely painful anguish often
expresses his state by saying that he is nothing but pure suffering
itself, or just as one might say of somebody entirely devoured
by passion that he is nothing but this passion, in the same way,
when some quality is attributed to God in absolute measure, He
appears actually to become the quality in substantial form.

[Here one might say that man's fundamental religious spirit
is left alone with that which it has seized from empirical reality
and has raised to transcendent heights, and thus can remove it
from the limitations and relativity to which it is subject in the
empirical sphere.] Thus the idea that the world forms an absolute unity with no relativizing exterior forces—though demonstrable only very imperfectly in light of the empirical evidence
to which we have access—finds its expression in a self-sufficient
being that we call God: only a limited and relative being requires a bearer that exists in addition to fulfilling this function;
but an unconditional being, freed of all constraints, can cast off
these fetters. Depending on the kind of empirical material that

presents itself to this inner religious urge toward absolute unity, God might be the unity of the world as a whole, the unity of specific domains of physical nature, or the unity of the group. The social interactions of the group inspire the creation of this transcendent conception of unity, just as the feeling of the mystical association of all being does so in the world as a whole and just as the similarity of related phenomena does so in physical nature. From the standpoint of Christian religious culture, this genesis of ideas of God may seem fanciful and restricted, since it makes the deity appear as an absolutization of sociological unity. From a Christian perspective the deity is, on the one hand, the God of all being, especially of spiritual being, and the separation inherent in the nature of the social group is inapplicable and irrelevant in this Christian conception. Indeed, such separation is antagonistic to the very idea of such a deity and would be elevated to a universal concept of humankind. On the other hand, the Christian God is the God of the individual because the line that extends from the individual to God does not first pass through the intermediate stage of the group. [The individual is fully responsible for himself before God; such responsibility is reduced to an endurable measure only by Christ's death on the individual's behalf.] The purely sociological mediation is both too narrow and too broad for the Christian concept of God.

The ancient and the ethnic worlds have a completely different perspective, however, because the god of any self-contained group is its own. He looks after *them* and punishes *them;* the gods of other groups are accepted as equally real. Any particular group not only would not claim that its god should become the god of other groups; it would regard such an idea as an encroachment on its own sense of religious possession and would usually firmly reject the practical consequences [though the reverse phenomenon clearly perpetuates the same idea, as when the Assyrian kings waged war both to extend their own power and to spread the recognition and worship of their gods among other peoples]. The jealous possession of a politically defined god, which would be begrudged another tribe as would a powerful leader or a miracle-working sorcerer, is the positive extension or exaggeration of that tolerance that essentially characterizes all particularist religions. As soon as the god has a relationship with the community of his faithful, to the exclusion of all others, religiosity must accept that other gods exist alongside him—the gods of other groups. His own followers, of course, should not believe in any other gods, not because these do not exist but, to put it somewhat paradoxically, because of their very existence (otherwise the risk would not be so great), for they are not the true and genuine gods for *this* particular group. This interdiction is exactly consistent with any other political prohibition: group members are not to defect to another group and are not under any circumstances to break away from the existing social unit.

Even the Brahmins, with their pantheistically colored religion, show the following tolerance, which is the counterpart to their particularism: when confronted with certain objections to their religion by Christian missionaries, they replied that their religion probably did not suit all peoples, but that it was the right one for them. In view of this solidarity of the god with the social unit, which is always specific, Christianity brought about an enormous revolution through its denial of the existence of all gods other than its own, not only for itself but universally. Its God is not only the God of its followers but the God of all being. Thus not only does Christianity lack that exclusivity, that jealous possession of a god; it also and contrastingly must, if it is to be consistent, seek to have its God recognized by every soul, because He is also the God of these souls. Their conversion to Christianity is merely the confirmation of something that is already true. "He who is not for me is against me": this concept is one of the greatest historical turning points in the sociology of religion. If a person believed in Wotan or in Vitzliputzli, this did not mean in any way that he was "against" Zeus or Baal: each god was of concern only to his followers and each community was of concern only to its own god. No god encroached on the sphere of another by requiring to be worshipped by another community.

It is the Christian God who first extended His realm to include both those who believe in Him and those who do not. Of all [supratheoretical] life forces, He was the first to transcend that exclusivity of the social group which had thus far embraced all of its individual members' interests within a single temporal and spatial unit. For this reason it is impossible for a relationship to the Christian God to exist indifferently alongside the relationship of other men to other gods. This would in fact be a positive infringement of the claim to totality that derives from His all-encompassing absoluteness; to believe in other gods would mean rebelling against Him, because in fact He is the God of the unfaithful as well. [When the other god is not simply the other man's god but a false god—that is, one that is completely nonexistent—tolerance is just as much a logical contradiction as intolerance would be to the particularist religions. Of course, a new tolerance is born of this: the very absoluteness and indisputable oneness of the divine principle allows for a diversity of paths by which to reach this one and only God.

The particularist religions can be tolerant with regard to the ultimate content of religion, the concept of god. In terms of his intimacy and closeness, however, the individuality of each person's relationship to him, such religions cannot recognize more than one way of reaching him: he can be reached only by certain particular sacrifices, prayers, or types of behavior. Christianity, on the other hand, is intolerant in regard to the definitive content of religion but is able to admit an incomparable breadth of activities and inner states that are pleasing to God. Once a single path to the Most High has been chosen, it may be dogmatically intolerant to the highest degree. Christianity as a principle, however, must allow this multiplicity of paths to God as a counterbalance to His very unity, because this unity is absolute. The general historical development of the Christian principle has indeed put this idea into practice. The Anabaptist sects, for example, and later Calvinism, demonstrate this correlation: in these groups the quality of religiousness emerges as or by means of divine election and awakening. By thus rejecting all *outward* symptoms, the community must claim for its inner states the absolute tolerance of other authorities (for example, of the state) and must practice the same tolerance toward neighboring communities. This is not only external but also linked closely in a causal sense with the inner intolerance and the uncompromising quality that are logically and psychologically characteristic of such religions based on the doctrine of election. Intolerance of this kind never can arise in relation to gods that embody the unity of the social group.] It *is* just as impossible that the god of an African tribe might be that of the Chinese as that the parents of an African might be those of a Chinese person, or that the political system of a self-contained group *as such* might simultaneously serve another self-contained group.

It might be that the unity of the divine being, as embodied in [that particularist]-societal form, is the preliminary stage of the absolute form it takes in Christianity. If this is the case, this development is one of those which represent a negation and a reversal of all the phenomena that have led up to it, once it has reached its definitive stage. The all-encompassing unity of the Christian God goes beyond the societal limitations within which that concept of unity first emerged. The passing of earthly relativities into transcendent absoluteness often renders the quality of their content the very opposite of what it was originally. The religious affections, for example, are essentially determined by the man of faith's feeling that he is a *distinct* entity from his God: love and humbleness, mercy and rejection, prayer and obedience—all require the existence of another being, as has been shown in a different context. In the state of religious ecstasy, for example, this sense of separateness may appear to be suspended, but in fact even ecstasy is no more than a reaching out from the intolerability of complete separation into the impossibility of complete oneness. It is still the case that the concept of God as the absolute substance and force of being apparently compels us to the consequence of pantheism, in which any separateness of individual existence is entirely suspended. Indeed, the more the soul struggles to attain unbroken unity with God, the further, deeper, and more blissful it feels itself to be. If it were to attain *total* unity, however, by achieving unrestrained fusion with Him, the soul itself would stand in a void; for any sense of religiousness always attaches itself to a distinct object vis à vis. Whereas the diminution of this distinctness enhances religious contentment and strength, its *absolute* suspension would cause all conceivable meaning and content of religiousness to sink into nothing. Thus the idea of God may have grown upwards from its sociological [prefiguration] to gain an ever-increasing breadth of significance. Yet as soon as this process reaches its final stage with the absolute God of Christianity, its content suddenly changes into the opposite of that societal character which provided the exclusivity on which the idea of God depended originally.

Why, however, does group unity have this tendency to cloak itself in the form of transcendence and to equip itself with emotional qualities of a religious nature? It may well be that this synthesis of individuals in the higher form of group unity is often perceived by the individual—with a greater or lesser degree of consciousness—as some kind of miracle. In this context individual existence experiences itself as involved in an interplay of irresistible forces and to be surrounded by a set of powers that can apparently not be accounted for by its single elements, reaching beyond all of them with a temporality and dynamism that defies calculation. Law and custom, language and tradition—all of what has been called objectified mind confronts the individual as an enormously rich source in which it is impossible to distinguish the share of the individual; hence it does not appear to have developed from individual contributions at all but as the product of this mysterious unity which is subject to supraindividual norms beyond the sum of its individual elements. Just as in the case of man's reaction to the natural world, here too it is the sense of practical and theoretical helplessness that calls forth the religious response. And this religious reaction does not visibly attach itself to the group as the sum of coexisting human beings, for they are immediately palpable in a way that robs them of any sense of mystery and would limit the mind to the empirical sphere. Instead, religious inspiration is drawn from the fact that this sum of individual lives is more than just a *sum,* that it develops powers that cannot be traced within the individual alone, and that a greater unity grows from these units. The belonging of a god to a specific group, the preservation of religion as a concern of the whole group, the punishment of the individual's religious offenses by the group, and the general liability of the group for such sins toward the god—all these typical phenomena show that the deity is, as it were, the transcendent location of the powers of the group. The interactive processes *between* the group elements, which constitute its unity in a functional sense [and thus bear a symbolic formal relationship to the mysterious unity of religious being], have taken on their own distinct existence as the god. The dynamics of group life are borne up by the momentum of religious feeling and are projected beyond the materials and agents of those dynamics into the transcendent sphere. From there these social powers confront all the relative details as an absolute principle. The old idea that God is the absolute, whereas everything human is relative, thereby acquires a new significance: it is the relations between human beings that find their substantive and ideal expression in the idea of the deity.

[Looking back over the investigations thus concluded, one can distinguish two main motifs. Although these cannot be combined easily, it would be quite possible to link them systematically if it were thought to be important. The first main point is that the objective, mental form of religion has appeared as the product of religious *life.* The latter is a process or a way of being, whereas the content or the "articles of faith" of religion

are drawn from the facts of worldly existence. It is characteristic
of such religious life that it becomes objectified in the form of
the *absolute,* drawing its content from social facts (as well as from
other facts of empirical existence) and projecting these in absolute form into the transcendent sphere. In doing so, it acquires
the constantly proven ability to cast a reflection on the relative
facts of the earthly sphere, investing them with a sublimity and
grandeur and drawing out their essence. The old observation
that the gods are an absolutization of the empirical sphere thus
loses the sensualist connotations it had during the Enlightenment. The empirical would never have become transcendent—
as the Enlightenment view naively supposes it would—unless
the religious motive of life had been an underlying concept and
force, extending its empirical objects out beyond themselves according to *its own* law, not according to some law to be found
in the *empirical sphere.* Religiosity follows this path, traversing a
sphere that is external to itself, employing elements from this external sphere to assume its form but leaving behind the specific
substance of this alien material to achieve its own purity within
the purified form of the latter. Ultimately, however, the end of
the path is perhaps never quite reached. Instead, "religion" as a
finished, objectified product seems to carry material pieces of
this external sphere wherever it goes. Religiosity as a quality of
spiritual being, *the religious life process,* has the remarkable fate,
almost reminiscent of Hegel's dialectical scheme, of being required to go out itself to acquire a form from some external
source, though this form is no more than an objectified manifestation of itself. As we have said, however, it suffers from the in-
ability to shake off this otherness, once it has become associated
with it. Religion in its truly pure stage is doomed to develop
only by an infinitely long process, because religiosity remains
fused with *forms* of the earthly, rationalist, social-empirical material through which objective religion came into being, while
still enduring the presence of random particles of its *matter.*

It seems to me that it is possible to apply the concept of

"progressive development" to religion only in the following way: not that a more perfect religion emerges, but that religion as such acquires a more perfect, more purely religious form. I will not attempt to deal with the methodological problem of whether "religion" as such may be regarded in any way as a concrete subject that "develops" from fetishism and ancestor worship to Christianity. It may be that a person's estimation of his own faith as the absolute highest leads him to see this faith as the highest faith in a relative sense, at the top of an upward progression leading toward it. This view, however, would assume the questionable notion of "imperfect" religion. I admit that I no more believe in imperfect religions than I do in imperfect artistic styles. Of course, some spiritual motives or objectified forms are religious in intention but are not fully developed religions; to put it another way, these religions are impure mixtures, as mentioned earlier, where religiousness has not yet acquired a pure, objective form. Yet if these phenomena are perfectly religious, then they are "perfect religion," just as the painting of the trecento is art as perfect as later art, even though it displays no shade, no natural movement, and no perspective, as do later paintings. Giotto simply *intended* something different from Raphael or Velázquez. Indeed, if it can be claimed in any way that art is "perfect" in the sense that it is formed by no motifs other than artistic ones and that primitive sensory impulses, preoccupation with coincidental reality, or influences from other areas of interest do not appear visually, then every intention to produce art is equal to every other. Any question of perfection or imperfection can be related only to the question of whether individual genius is greater or lesser.

Yet if we consider style as such, the relation of artistic intent to the means of expression, the complex unity of what is to be depicted—here it is not possible to apply the concept of the development from the imperfect to the perfect. On the contrary, what Schopenhauer said of the general nature of art can be said of the individual style or era: art "always achieves its goal." If the drawings of Africans are more "imperfect" than the drawings of Rodin, this is so, first, because they are not only art but also a result of the mere pleasure of imitation, the product of a childlike play instinct and fetishist tendencies; second, because the individual artistic ability in such cases, as expressed through style, cannot match that of a great artist. Only in this sense can one speak of a scale ranging from more imperfect to perfect religion; religion can become more pure only in itself, freer of alien impulses or worlds, and can mold itself more exclusively within the religious category as such. But if it is really religion, it always "achieves its goal"—whether ancestor worship or polytheism, pantheistic mysticism or clearly defined theism. The differences in perfection lie only in the quantities of depth and breadth, as it were, the measure of power and passion with which the various individuals live out these religious styles and practical potentialities of religion. In short, the historical development from the more imperfect to the perfect is by no means an exhaustive epistemological scheme for the significance of religion, even though modern evolutionism and Christian apologetics themselves conspire toward such idealization.

This motif of the sequence *religiosity—social phenomenon— objective religion* (not intended, of course, as a temporal sequence) was occasionally accompanied by a second motif. That infrequency was imposed by the more speculative nature of this motif and by its unconduciveness to historical exemplification. Whereas the first motif derives from the religious quality of the spiritual process, it might be possible to postulate processes and states that are *formal* in a purer sense. They manifest themselves in religious phenomena on the one hand and in social phenomena on the other, and determine the configuration of the content of religion, thereby giving rise to the analogies and interconnections between the two spheres of which these pages have cited examples. Here again, this motif should be regarded not as a temporal sequence of influences, but as a reconstruction of spiritual unity with elements whose interrelationship demonstrates the *meaning* of this unity according to what might be called the logic of psychology. Let us not labor under any illusion: nobody yet has successfully attempted an exact genetic investigation of the phenomenon of religion as such. All explanations of the "origin" of religion—that it grew out of fear or love, out of need or the self's supraindividual consciousness, out of piety or a sense of dependence, or whatever other ideas—all of these omit the crucial question of why such empirical feelings suddenly progress to a religious stage of development. The obvious answer—accurate enough as far as it goes—is that a certain increase in the quantity of these feelings makes them acquire an entirely new quality, and that a certain *threshold* marks the boundary of religious consciousness. Yet this answer still evades the question of why this new quality is necessarily that of *religion*.

If one looks very closely, all ostensible attempts to trace the origin of religiousness always tacitly assume its preexistence; it will thus be better to recognize it as a primary quality that cannot be derived from anything else. Seen in this light, it is far easier to understand the relationship between religion itself and these ostensible origins, for it seems to me that all these factors—to express the idea in a rather vague and unsystematic way—are formal states of tension, general psychic impulses that give a certain direction, rhythm, and synthesis to the qualitatively more definite processes within the psyche. Of course (and I can allude to this only briefly here), all these factors—love, fear, dependence, dedication, and so on—are too specific. One would perhaps have to draw on more general, more purely functional impulses and on fundamental spiritual relations in order to project psychic structure onto a conceptual plane in keeping with the psychological logic mentioned here. These more fundamental categories would then determine the nature of specific feelings, destinies, and interests, whether religious, social, artistic, or ethical. We still have no way of expressing in psychological terms this tension and release of spiritual being: the rhythmic change in its temperature, the general dynamics of passion, disappointment, resistance, equilibrium. Even if such description were possible, it would still fail to explain the underlying *causes* of those major categories which formed the starting point of this essay, each capable of creating its own world image: practical life and art, knowledge and religion, moral judgment and societal syntheses. But such description would help us comprehend the real and conceptual relationships between the worldviews thus formed, their parallel processes, and the preformations by which they influence one another, of which a few examples relating to one specific area are presented in this essay.

I have stressed repeatedly that we are dealing here solely with the structural meaning of religion as a spiritual phenomenon. In doing so, I intend to deter the reader from seeking within these pages any statement regarding the objective, suprapsychological existence of the objects of religion. The question of whether religious content, of which this essay has dealt only with the formative psychic process, also exists in reality is an issue that must be kept distinct from our present inquiry in the strictest methodological fashion. This distinction perhaps becomes most urgent when applied to historical knowledge concerning religion. By concluding with a rejection of the misinterpretation so frequently associated with such knowledge, I believe I will take the most effective stand against any such falsification that might threaten the investigations pursued here.]

Even if we succeed in understanding the emergence of religion as an event in the life of humanity deriving from the spiritual preconditions of this very life, we still do not touch on the problem of whether the reality located outside human thought actually contains the empirical counterpart and affirmation of this psychic reality. But not only is the significance of religion in the objective sphere completely independent of any postulations about the origins of the idea of religion; also unaffected is the status of religion in the subjective sphere, its emotional significance—that is, the most deeply spiritual effects of the idea of a deity. Here we touch on the most severe misconception to which all historical and psychological deduction is subject, [and also by which any attempt to trace the spiritual content of ideal values] is threatened. Many still feel that an ideal loses its attraction, that the dignity of an emotion is degraded if its origin is no longer an incomprehensible miracle, a creation out of nothing—as if comprehension of its development affected the value of a thing, [as if analysis of its constituent elements were to call into question the value of its vital unity,] as if lowliness of origin were to detract from the loftiness of the goal already achieved, or as if the sober simplicity of its several [components] could destroy the significance of the product that emerges from the creative interaction and interlinking of these elements. Such is the foolish and confused notion that the dignity of humanity is profaned by tracing man's origin to the lower animals, as if that dignity did not depend on what man really *is,* regardless of his origin. But precisely the persons who hope to preserve the dignity of religion by denying its historical-psychological origin must be reproached with weakness of religious consciousness. The subjective certainty and emotional depth of such religiousness surely must be limited if the knowledge of its origin and development endangers or even makes the slightest difference in its worth. For just as the most genuine and most profound love for a human being is not affected by subsequent evidence concerning its causes—indeed, as its triumphant strength is revealed by its outlasting all such causes—so the strength of subjective religiousness is revealed only by the assurance that it has within itself, and which gives it a depth and an intensity entirely beyond the causes to which investigation might trace it.

# References

Comte, A. 1842. *Cours de philosophie positive.* Vol. 6. Paris: Lagrange.

Dörr-Backes, F., and L. Nieder (eds.). 1995. *Georg Simmel Between Modernity and Postmodernity.* Würzburg: Königshausen & Neumann.

Durkheim, E. 1893. *De la division du travail social.* Paris: Alcan.

———. 1912. *Les formes élémentaires de la vie religieuse.* Paris: Alcan.

Etzkorn, P. 1968. *Georg Simmel: The Conflict in Modern Culture and Other Essays,* translated, with an introduction by K. Peter Etzkorn. New York: Teachers College Press, Teachers College, Columbia University.

Levine, D. N. 1957. "Simmel and Parsons: Two Approaches to the Study of Society." Doctoral dissertation, Division of the Social Sciences, University of Chicago.

Marx, K. (1844) 1985. "Contribution to the Critique of Hegel's Philosophy of Law: Introduction." Pp. 38–52 in K. Marx and F. Engels, *On Religion.* Moscow: Progress Publishers.

Miller, E. M., and D. J. Jaffe. 1984. "Georg Simmel: On Religion from the Point of View of the Theory of Knowledge." *The New England Sociologist* 5(1): 61–75.

Rosenthal, C. 1959. *Georg Simmel: Sociology of Religion,* translated from the German. New York: Wisdom Library.

Simmel, G. (1892, 1905) 1977. *The Problems of the Philosophy of History,* translated, edited, and introduced by Guy Oakes. New York: Free Press.

———. (1892) 1983. *Einleitung in die Moralwissenschaft.* Aalen: Scientia.

———. 1898. "Zur Soziologie der Religion." *Neue Deutsche Rundschau* 9: 111–23.

———. (1900) 1978. *The Philosophy of Money,* translated by Tom Bottomore and David Frisby. London: Henley.

———. 1902. "Beiträge zur Erkenntnistheorie der Religion." *Zeitschrift für Philosophie und philosophische Kritik* 119 (902): 11–22. Reprinted 1984, pp. 100–109 in *Das Individuum und die Freiheit: Essais.* Berlin: Klaus Wagenbach.

———. (1903) 1971. "The Metropolis and Mental Life." Pp. 324–39 in

*Georg Simmel: On Individuality and Social Forms,* edited by Donald Levine. Chicago: University of Chicago Press.

———. 1903a. "De la religion au point de vue de la théorie de la connaissance." Pp. 319–37 in *Bibliothèque du congrès international de philosophie,* Vol. 2: *Morale générale.* Paris: Librairie Armand Colin.

———. 1903b. "Vom Heil der Seele." *Das freie Wort* 2: 533–38. Reprinted 1984, pp. 114–20 in *Das Individuum und die Freiheit: Essais.* Berlin: Klaus Wagenbach.

———. 1904. "Die Gegensätze des Lebens und die Religion." *Das freie Wort* 4(8): 305–12.

———. 1905. "A Contribution to the Sociology of Religion." *American Journal of Sociology* 11(3): 359–76.

———. 1907. "Das Christentum und die Kunst." *Der Morgen, Wochenzeitschrift für deutsche Kultur* 1(8): 234–43.

———. 1909. "Beitrag Georg Simmels zu 'Religiöse Grundgedanken und Moderne Wissenschaft: Eine Umfrage.'" *Nord und Süd* 128(383): 366–69.

———. 1911a. "Die Persönlichkeit Gottes." Pp. 207–26 in *Philosophische Kultur: Gesammelte Essays von Georg Simmel.* Leipzig: Klinkhardt.

———. 1911b. "Das Problem der religiösen Lage." Pp. 327–40 in *Weltanschauung: Philosophie und Religion in Darstellungen von Wilhelm Dilthey u.a.,* edited by M. Frischeisen-Köhler. Berlin: Reichl. Reprinted 1911, pp. 227–41 in *Philosophische Kultur: Gesammelte Essays von Georg Simmel.* Leipzig: Klinkhardt.

———. 1912. *Die Religion.* 2nd ed. Frankfurt: Rutten & Loening.

———. 1914. "Rembrandts religiöse Kunst." *Frankfurter Zeitung,* June 30 and July 1.

———. (1916) 1919. *Rembrandt: Ein Kunstphilosophischer Versuch.* 2nd ed. Leipzig: Kurt Wolff Verlag.

———. 1918. *Der Konflikt der modernen Kultur: Ein Vortrag.* Leipzig: Duncker & Humblot.

———. 1993. *Saggi di sociologia della religione,* edited by Roberto Cipriani and with an introduction by Horst J. Helle. Rome: Edizioni Borla.

Weber, M. 1904. "Die protestantische Ethik und der 'Geist' des Kapitalismus." *Archiv für Sozialwissenschaft und Sozialpolitik* 20(1): 1–51.

———. 1978. *Economy and Society.* Berkeley: University of California Press.

Wolff, K. H. (1950) 1964. *The Sociology of Georg Simmel,* translated, edited, and introduced by K. H. Wolff. New York: Free Press.

————. 1963. "Book Review: Georg Simmel, *Sociology of Religion.*" *Journal for the Scientific Study of Religion* 2(2): 258–59.

Yinger, J. M. 1957. *Religion, Society and the Individual: An Introduction to the Sociology of Religion.* New York: Macmillan.

# INDEX

Absolute, God as, 171–75, 189, 200, 205–8
Africa, 206, 211
Ahriman, 130
American Indians, 29
Anabaptists, 205–6
Ancestor worship, 210–11
Angelico, Fra, 82, 90
Arabs, 112, 157, 168–9, 178, 181
Art, 65–97, 141, 163, 199; ancient, 74
Assyrians, 112, 181, 203
Astarte, 112, 181
Attitude, xi–xiii
Augustine, xii, 117

Baal, 7, 112, 204
Bach, Johann Sebastian, 89
Bartolommeo, Fra, 80
Beardsley, Aubrey, 88
Belief, 127–33, 166–70
Bible, 88, 94, 121
Body, portrayed in art, 68
Botticelli, Sandro, 71
Brahman, 7, 204
Bridging the rift, xii–xiii
Buber, Martin, xiv, xvii
Buddha, 68, 86, 101
Buddhism, xvii, 159–60, 191
Byzantine art, 79

Calvinism, 83, 206

Canaanites, 112, 180
Catholicism, xvii, 19, 78, 83, 114
Cecilia, Saint, 73
Center, xiv
China, 154, 206
Christ. *See* Jesus Christ
Christianity, xvi–xvii, 101, 132, 201, 210–11; traditions of, 3–4; deity of, 7–8, 34, 53, 59, 69–73, 75–76, 130, 171, 203–7; salvation in, 30, 32–35, 194–96, 198; emphasis on renunciation, 41; and art, 65–97; and individual, 114; and social obligations, 159–60; unity in, 175–79, 190–91
Christmas, 178
Communion, 113, 178
Competition, 177–78
Comte, Auguste, xv
Content, xiii–xiv, 31, 107, 124–26, 129–30
Contradictions of life, 36–44
Cultural forms, 24–25
Cusanus, Nicolaus, 36
Custom, 103, 105, 152–53, 207
Cyprian, 175

Dante Alighieri, 95
Depression, 75
*Dharma,* 105, 152
Dilthey, Wilhelm, xvi–xvii